LOCKING UP THE RANGE

PACIFIC STUDIES IN PUBLIC POLICY

The Public School Monopoly
A Critical Analysis of Education and the State in American Society
Edited by Robert B. Everhart
With a foreword by Clarence B. Karier

Resolving the Housing Crisis
Government Policy, Decontrol, and the Public Interest
Edited with an introduction
by M. Bruce Johnson

FORTHCOMING

Impoverishing America
The Political Economy of the Transfer Society

Natural Resources
Myths and Management

Firearms and Violence
Issues of Regulation

Inflation or Deflation?
Prospects for Capital Formation and Employment

Water in the West
Scarce Resource Allocation, Property Rights, and the Environment

Forestlands
Public and Private

Rationing Health Care
Medical Licensing in the U.S.

For further information on the Pacific Institute's program and a catalog of publications, please contact:

PACIFIC INSTITUTE
FOR PUBLIC POLICY RESEARCH

635 Mason Street
San Francisco, California 94108

LOCKING UP THE RANGE
Federal Land Controls and Grazing

GARY D. LIBECAP

PACIFIC STUDIES IN PUBLIC POLICY
PACIFIC INSTITUTE FOR PUBLIC POLICY RESEARCH
San Francisco, California

BALLINGER PUBLISHING COMPANY
Cambridge, Massachusetts
A Subsidiary of Harper & Row, Publishers, Inc.

International Standard Book Number: ISBN 0-88410-382-X

Library of Congress Catalog Card Number: 81-12709

Printed in the United States of America

Library of Congress Cataloging in Publication Data

Libecap, Gary D.
  Locking up the range.

  Bibliography: p.
  Includes index.
    1. Grazing districts—United States.   2. United States—Public lands.
3. United States.   Bureau of Land Management.   I. Title.
HD241.L5   333.74'17'0973   81-12709
ISBN 0-88410-382-X   AACR2

PACIFIC INSTITUTE

FOR PUBLIC POLICY RESEARCH

The Pacific Institute for Public Policy Research is an independent, tax-exempt, research and educational organization. The Institute's program is designed to broaden public understanding of the nature and effects of market processes and government policy.

With the bureaucratization and politicization of modern society, scholars, business and civic leaders, the media, policymakers, and the general public have too often been isolated from meaningful solutions to critical public issues. To facilitate a more active and enlightened discussion of such issues, the Pacific Institute sponsors in-depth studies into the nature and possible solutions to major social, economic, and environmental problems. Undertaken regardless of the sanctity of any particular government program, or the customs, prejudices, or temper of the times, the Institute aims to ensure that alternative approaches to currently problematic policy areas are fully evaluated, the best remedies discovered, and these findings made widely available. The results of this work are published as books and monographs, and form the basis for numerous conference and media programs.

Through this program of research and commentary, the Institute seeks to evaluate the premises and consequences of government policy, and provide the foundations necessary for constructive policy reform.

CONTENTS

LIST OF FIGURES

LIST OF TABLES

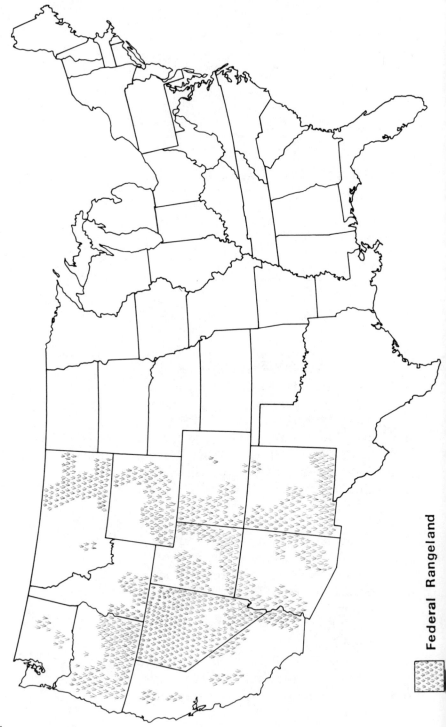

Federal Rangeland

FOREWORD

Since the 1960s long-run objectives in management of U.S. publicly owned rangelands have changed radically. These semiarid western lands cover a vest area of 174 million acres, larger than New England and the Middle-Atlantic states combined. Secure property rights to these lands were never assigned, and the experience common to the rest of the nation (Indian reservations apart) —economic development based upon exploitation of permanent private rights to real property—never were achieved fully in that huge region. What did occur remains an anomoly in the American national experience: a suboptimal use based upon uncertain tenure. That is precisely what the architects of our national land policy intended to avoid. Thomas Jefferson, planning the Northwest Ordinance of 1785, wrote that the federal government should sell all its vast domain to private owners, and then it should "never after, in any case, revert to the United States." What happened in the West was that a great fiefdom of undistributed land was left permanently in the hands of government, to become a base of bureaucratic power. That was what Jefferson wanted most to avoid—government ownership of the means of production.

But the founding fathers had no conception of the West in the 1780s when the basic land laws were drafted—laws as powerful as the federal constitution itself in shaping the country's ultimate destiny. Small family farms, mainly in quarter sections of 160 acres, could support a growing population in the Ohio Valley, but not in Nevada. The American wave of settlers and homesteaders exhausted itself on the edges and in the seams of the western deserts. There dry-land farming was sharply restricted and irrigation possibilities limited. The semiarid grasslands could only support livestock in herds of viable sizes on large-scale holdings. But the land policy, frozen forever in 36-square-mile townships and sections of 640 acres, was designed for family farms. The bureaucracy in charge, the old General Land Office, depended for its own existence, decade after decade, upon doling out the continent in 160-acre patches.

New laws like the Timber Culture Act (1873), the Desert Land Act (1877), and the Newlands Act (1902) were intended to encourage family farms larger than 160 acres, but still too small for livestock ranching. The early cattlemen used the open range by common-law prescriptive right: "first come, first served," with established rights protected in the future. That was upset by continued homesteading. In the late 1880s the system of range ranching developed: a deeded ranch purchased or homesteaded, supplemented by renewable grazing rights on the unclaimed public lands. Such arrangements made every rancher a potential free rider, since the common resource not claimed by one would be exploited by another. Improvements would not pay if they could be exploited by another. This was a blueprint for overgrazing and abusive exploitation. In theory a profit-maximizing rancher would not destroy his own estate by overgrazing it, but what of a common estate? Theory tells us and experience shows that common property rights tend to be overused.

Until the 1930s only temporary expedients to limit entry onto grazing lands could diminish such exploitation. And it was charged that overgrazing had produced waste and erosion. From 1934 to 1960 under the Taylor Grazing Act, local advisory boards of ranchers guided a fairly stable, "grandfathered" system of restricted user rights. Yet there were other players. In the background was a different sort of game—government growth and change together with bureaucratic maneuvering over control of the rangelands. By 1947 the Interior Department's present Bureau of Land Management had evolved from this rivalry, and in the 1970s the old-time conservationist interest was greatly augmented by demographic change and the emerging and politically vital environmental interest. The management objective shifted from grazing to multiuse "scientific" targets including natural balance of plants and restored wildlife. The ranching interest was weakened and centrally directed government planning for the range gained ascendency.

Great shifts of wealth and income emerge from these policy changes. There could be no other results. Rangeland yield is a potential economic rent. Who will capture it? The actual rent is created by the government permit exploited by private capital and effort, and division of rent is between grantor and grantee. The uncertain tenure produces disequilibrium uses and thus extraordinary rent-seeking behavior. Shifts in policy affect the returns of all players, users, bureaucracy, and, residually, the nonparticipating public, nominal owners of the rangeland asset.

Professor Libecap uses the rangeland in this study as a fascinating laboratory for economic analysis. His work illuminates clear and simple tests for modern property rights theory, the theory of bureaucratic behavior (including interbureau competition), the theory of regulatory capture, and modern theories of regulatory change. His own preference is for an optimal economic solution, final distribution of the rangeland rights to private owners in secure and permanent tenures. He argues that any other solution must yield a future of social waste on the rangelands. His analysis must stand as a challenge to those who support the present movement toward permanent government control and planning of the rangelands' future.

Jonathan R. T. Hughes
Northwestern University
Evanston, Illinois
April 1981

1 AN OVERVIEW
Bureaucratic Opposition to the Assignment of Property Rights to the Western Range

The vast public rangelands managed by the Bureau of Land Management are currently far below their production potential. The reasons for this are varied, but the principal causes are a legacy of unwise and uncontrolled use from the last century and a history of inadequate public investment in this century. Improving the productivity of these lands today is complicated, in part, by the real conflict in many cases (and a perceived conflict in almost all cases) between the immediate economic needs of individual livestock operators—the principal range users—and the longer-range interests of the operator, his community, and the Nation as a whole.

U.S. Department of the Interior (1979:iii)

The quoted passage captures the current controversy between the Bureau of Land Management (BLM) within the Interior Department and western ranchers who depend upon federal land for raising livestock. The BLM administers 174 million acres of land (an area larger than the combined Mid-Atlantic and New England states) in the eleven far western states. Usage rights to this vast acreage are granted ranchers through grazing permits issued by the secretary of the interior. The privileges conveyed by the permits are being sharply curtailed as the bureau broadens its regulatory powers and assumes a broader managerial role over western lands. The agency

1

argues that increased regulation of private use is necessary to balance immediate market pressures for livestock grazing with long-term conservation needs. It asserts that ranchers, in their desire to maximize profits, have an inherent short-term bias in stocking decisions, overgrazing the land to increase current returns, and neglecting conservation.

Despite a lack of theoretical support or significant empirical evidence, this notion has been used to justify major intervention by the Bureau of Land Management in land allocation and use. Under plans being implemented throughout its jurisdiction, the agency is imposing sharp reductions in the number of livestock allowed on federal land (in some cases 30 percent or more); restricting pasture use; and reassigning forage to wildlife and wilderness. Those actions and uncertainty regarding future ones are disrupting the range livestock industry, imposing wealth losses on permit holders, and, more importantly, reducing the contribution of the range resource to total production. BLM lands commonly form an integral part of western ranches, with federal lands often exceeding 60 percent of total acreage. The enormity of the area involved under BLM management and the vulnerability of western states to bureaucratic regulation are revealed in the following statistics: the agency administers 23 percent of the acreage in the eleven far western states; nearly 70 percent of Nevada; over 40 percent of Utah; over 20 percent of Wyoming, Oregon, and Idaho; and nearly 20 percent of Arizona, California, New Mexico, and Colorado. In only Montana and Washington does the BLM control less than 10 percent of the land (U.S. Department of the Interior 1976). Legislatures in states most affected by bureau actions, particularly Nevada, have responded by calling for the divestiture of western lands from federal ownership. That reaction has been termed the sagebrush rebellion.

This study shows that the current controversy is a long-standing one; that ranchers and the Interior Department have competed for control of the western range for over one hundred years because secure property rights have never been granted. Until they are, contention between the two will continue and tenure to the range will remain confused and uncertain. Insecure tenure encourages overstocking and discourages investments in improvements such as fences and wells. Indeed, "the legacy of unwise and uncontrolled use" of rangeland cited in the opening passage of this chapter was due to a federally imposed lack of well-defined property rights, not inherent short-run biases of ranchers. The existing arrangement of bureaucratically assigned use privileges is not a satisfactory alternative to formal property rights. Such privileges are necessarily unstable as the bureau adjusts them to meet changing political conditions. Further, formal grazing privileges assign rights to use the resource, but not to the resource itself, and that reduces the incentive of individuals to maximize the rental value of the range. The study also challenges the notion that Interior Department policies are principally motivated in the public interest. The model of bureaucratic behavior outlined in chapter 2 argues that the department is importantly guided by self-interest needs to expand budgets and staffs.

The history of competition between ranchers and the Interior Department began in the 1880s. Because of arid conditions and low carrying capacity, stock owners made prior appropriation claims to acreage well in excess of the 160 acres allowed by the Homestead Act. As chapters 3 and 4 show, the claims of ranchers posed barriers to the high plains agricultural settlement endorsed by the Interior Department and its General Land Office (GLO) division. The GLO rejected assertions that more than 160 acres were necessary for viable ranch operations, opposed major modification of the land laws, and resisted efforts in Congress to recognize the informal holdings of ranchers. Their fences were removed, and common property conditions emerged. Predictable overgrazing followed, accompanied by severe wind and water erosion, low livestock quality, and high animal mortality rates.

The 1934 Taylor Grazing Act changed the emphasis of federal land policy from disposal of lands to bureaucratic administration of them. The act granted jurisdiction over the remaining unreserved range to the Interior Department, and it assigned stock owners formal grazing permits subject to bureaucratic regulation, initially by the Grazing Service, and after 1946 by the Bureau of Land Management. Contention between permittees and the BLM has centered on the extent of grazing privileges granted ranchers and the regulatory role of the bureau. Those issues are addressed in chapters 5 and 6. Chapter 6 also points out that bureaucratic management, which focuses on biological goals such as maximum sustained yield, reduces the present value of the range if ranchers are prevented from adjusting stocking levels to changing market conditions.

The recurring theme of this study is that the Interior Department has continually influenced land policy to advance its administrative and regulatory role. The department has promoted legislation it favored, and used its discretion in implementing the laws. This view contrasts with the assertions of the department and convention studies by Calef (1960), Clawson (1950, 1971), Clawson and Held (1957), Foss (1960), Gates (1968), Peffer (1951), and Voigt (1976). Those authors generally describe Interior as acting in the public interest in carrying out homestead legislation in the nineteenth century and in conserving rangeland in the twentieth in face of opposition from livestock owners. Because they ignore the influence of narrow, bureaucratic goals, those studies are unsatisfactory for understanding the development of U.S. land policies; the continuing lack of formal property rights to rangeland; and the economic effects of uncertain tenure and bureaucratic regulation. Those are the issues that underlie the sagebrush rebellion, and they are examined in detail in the following chapters.

The call at the end of this study for private property rights for more efficient rangeland use in the United States is underscored by worldwide concern for the condition of rangelands. It is not surprising that 75 percent of the world's grazing lands which are facing depletion do not have secure tenure arrangements (Williams et al. 1968). Common property conditions in many areas are leading to the overintensive harvest results predicted by Gordon in 1954. What is surprising is the suggested remedy. Williams and his associates, for instance, call for bureaucratic controls on land use similar to those imposed in the U.S. Yet, this study suggests that bureaucratic management is a costly and inefficient substitute for private property rights.

BIBLIOGRAPHY

Calef, Wesley. 1960. *Private Grazing on Public Lands: Studies of the Local Management of the Taylor Grazing Act.* Chicago: University of Chicago Press.

Clawson, Marion. 1950. *The Western Range Livestock Industry.* New York: McGraw-Hill.

————. 1971. *The Bureau of Land Management.* New York: Praeger Publications.

Clawson, Marion, and Burnell Held. 1957. *The Federal Lands, Their Use, and Management*. Baltimore: The Johns Hopkins Press.

Foss, Phillip O. 1960. *Politics and Grass*. Seattle: University of Washington Press.

Gates, Paul W. 1968. *History of Public Land Law Development*. Washington, D.C.: Public Land Law Review Commission.

Gordon, H. Scott. 1954. "The Economic Theory of a Common Property Resource: The Fishery." *Journal of Political Economy* 62:124–142.

Peffer, E. Louise. 1951. *The Closing of the Public Domain*. Stanford: Stanford University Press.

U.S. Department of the Interior, Bureau of Land Management. 1979. *Managing the Public Rangelands*. Washington, D.C.

————. 1976. *Public Lands Statistics*. Washington, D.C.

Voigt, William, Jr. 1976. *Public Grazing Lands*. New Brunswick, N.J.: Rutgers University Press.

Williams, Robert E.; B.W. Allred; Reginald M. Denis; Harold Paulsen, Jr. 1968. "Conservation, Development, and Use of the World's Rangelands." *Journal of Range Management* 21, no. 6 (November): 355–360.

2 ANALYTICAL FRAMEWORK
Bureaucrats, Ranchers, and Property Rights to the Range

Any theory of the behavior of bureaus that does not incorporate the personal preferences of bureaucrats will be relevant only in the most rigidly authoritarian environments.

Niskanen (1971:5)

This chapter provides an analytic framework for understanding federal land policy and the western range. It focuses on bureaucracies because of the important role the Department of the Interior has played in the disposal of land in the nineteenth century and the management of it in the twentieth. The analysis reveals that bureaucrats have sharply different incentives for land use than do ranchers, and that difference provides the groundwork for the continuing conflict over the range. The discussion of bureaucratic behavior builds on the work of De Alessi (1974), Lindsay (1976), Niskanen (1971, 1975), Peltzman (1976), Stigler (1971), Tullock (1965), and others who have examined the policies of administrative and regulatory agencies.

A BRIEF MODEL OF BUREAUCRATIC BEHAVIOR

The statutes passed by Congress regarding federal lands are general. The specifics of implementation are delegated to administrative

7

agencies such as the Interior Department and branches within it: homesteading and other land-claiming actions were processed by the General Land Office and, since 1934 central management of western lands has been through the Bureau of Land Management. The delegation of authority is crucial; it provides bureaucrats with important discretionary decision-making ability in expending funds, in developing programs, and in cultivating supportive lobby groups. The latter are particularly important. The various branches of the Interior Department are subject to annual congressional review of their budgets and staffing requests for the fiscal year. Favorable review depends, in part, upon lobbying by client groups. The failure of an agency to cultivate backing, particularly if it has adopted controversial policies, leaves it vulnerable to hostile monitoring by Congress. In exchange for their endorsement, lobbyists receive special privileges and other services from the agency.[1] Since there are numerous potential client groups, often with conflicting demands, bureaucratic managers must balance the expected political benefits from support of a particular group with the expected costs of adversely affecting others.[2] Well-organized and endowed groups offer greater influence, and hence are favored by the agency, but bureaucratic managers must select lobby supporters whose interests are compatible with the growth of the bureaucracy.[3]

Models of self-interested bureaucratic behavior stress the desire of bureaucrats to expand the administrative role, budget, and staffing of their agencies. A growing agency provides an environment for advancement to positions of greater authority and higher salaries. Because of the emphasis on growth, most models of bureaucratic behavior predict that bureau output will exceed that which is socially optimal and be provided at higher cost than if offered by private firms.[4] The discretion available to bureaucrats to broaden their agency's role, to subsidize favored groups, and to advertise for popular support for existing and new programs depends largely on the degree of congressional monitoring. Niskanen has argued that most members of Congress have little incentive to closely examine specific agency policies. The cost savings from intense review of bureau expenditures are spread across all voters, making per capita gains small and reducing the rewards received by the average senator or congressman.[5] Accordingly, congressional review committees which monitor administrative agencies become dominated by those whose states, districts, or client groups are directly affected by agency actions. Because of their influence in considering legislation and budget requests, members of review committees can pressure the bureau to be responsive to their constituents. However, bureaucrats have an advantage in controlling the information made available for the review process. Administrative agencies are often the only source of data necessary to evaluate proposed legislation or to measure bureaucratic performance. The selective release of pertinent data, then, can be used by bureaucrats to promote favored legislation (which they may have drafted) and to secure budget increases. The importance of controlling information in advancing the welfare of bureaucrats has been outlined by Lindsay (1976).

This view of self-interested, discretionary behavior by bureaucrats has important implications for production and wealth in the economy. Because they do not hold property rights to the resources they regulate, bureaucrats cannot capture the benefits nor bear the costs of their decisions. Accordingly, they do not have the same incentive that profit-maximizing firms do to increase the discounted net value of the resources under their control. Further, because bureaucrats are necessarily more sensitive to political than market forces, they will take action in response to political conditions, even though it reduces the total value of production.

THE INTERIOR DEPARTMENT, RANCHERS, AND THE RANGE

The central hypothesis of this study is that the Interior Department, motivated by self-interested goals, has competed since 1880 with ranchers for control of the western range. That competition has resulted in chronically insecure property rights to rangeland and associated waste and suboptimal land use.

In the nineteenth century, the General Land Office opposed the efforts of stock owners to define and enforce property rights to large areas of rangeland. The GLO budget was determined, in part, by annual claiming activity—total claims filed and acreage transferred. Moreover, officials at each land office received fee and commission payments for validating and processing claims, supplementing their income to a three-thousand-dollar limit.[6] Budgets, salaries, and long-term employment depended on the piecemeal disposal of federal land. Recognition of the holdings of ranchers, or even allowing for claims much larger than 160 acres, would have reduced the total number of claims to be processed and speeded the ultimate disposal of federal land.

In the twentieth century the Bureau of Land Management has attempted to manage federal rangeland following the successful model of the Forest Service, which has grown rapidly since its 1905 transfer to the Department of Agriculture. The BLM's budget depends upon a broad regulatory mandate. When land use decisions are left to permit holders with a minimal agency role, the budget is correspondingly small. When managerial functions are increased, however, there is justification for greater funding.

In both the nineteenth and twentieth centuries the competition between the Interior Department and ranchers has focused on two distinct but separate rental streams associated with rangeland. For ranchers, those rents equal the discounted net income from land use: to maximize returns they seek secure, exclusive decision-making authority in setting stocking levels and harvest rates, in controlling pasture use, in investing, and in transferring land to others. Such conditions are inconsistent with the reallocation efforts of the General Land Office or scientific management by the Bureau of Land Management; hence, conflict has resulted between ranchers and the agency. For the agencies the rental value of the land equals the discounted sum of budget appropriations. The broader the administrative and regulatory roles of the GLO and the BLM, the greater their appropriations, but the more tenuous the rights of ranchers.

The opposition of ranchers to GLO redistribution policies and tension between stock owners and the BLM contrast with the regulatory process described by Stigler (1971) and Peltzman (1976). They see mutual grounds for extensive contracting between administrative agencies and the regulated industry. However, for ranchers desiring formal recognition of their prior appropriation land claims, significant bureaucratic constraints serve largely to reduce their land rents.

The following chapter begins the application of this analytical framework by examining the problems faced by stock owners in securing property rights to rangeland.

NOTES

1. Stigler (1971:3-21) argues that regulatory agencies tend to be captured by the industry they regulate.
2. Peltzman (1976:211-240) stresses the cultivation of client groups and the trade offs involved.
3. Political power is discussed by Stigler (1975:137-141).
4. An outline of the predictions of various bureaucrats' behavior is provided by Orzechowski (1977:299-259).
5. The disincentive of congressmen and senators to monitor agencies is outlined by Niskanen (1975:417-643).
6. The use of fees to supplement income is discussed by the commissioner of the General Land Office in his *Annual Report* (U.S. Department of the Interior 1913).

BIBLIOGRAPHY

De Alessi, Louis. 1974. "An Economic Analysis of Government Ownership and Regulation: Theory and Evidence from the Electric Power Industry." *Public Choice* 19 (Fall):1-42.

Lindsay, Cotton M. 1976. "A Theory of Government Enterprise." *Journal of Political Economy* 84, no. 5:1061-1077.

Niskanen, William A. 1971. *Bureaucracy and Representative Government.* Chicago: Aldine.

_____.1975. "Bureaucracies and Politicians." *Journal of Law and Economics* 18, no. 3:617-643.

Orzechowski, William. 1977. "Economic Models of Bureaucracy: Survey, Extensions, and Evidence." In *Budgets and Bureaucrats: The Sources of Government Growth,* edited by Thomas E. Borcherding. Durham, N.C.: Duke University Press.

Peltzman, Sam. 1976. "Toward a More General Theory of Regulation." *Journal of Law and Economics* 19, no. 2:211-240.

Stigler, George. 1971. "The Theory of Economic Regulation." *Bell Journal of Economics and Management Science* 2:3-21.

_____. 1975. *The Citizen and the State.* Chicago: University of Chicago Press.

Tullock, George. 1965. *The Politics of Bureaucracy.* Washington, D.C.: Public Affairs Press.

U.S. Department of the Interior, General Land Office. 1913. *Annual Report of the Commissioner.* Washington, D.C.

3 OPEN RANGE—COSTS AND INFORMAL PROPERTY RIGHTS ARRANGEMENTS

There is perhaps no darker chapter nor greater tragedy in the history of land occupancy and use in the United States than the story of the western range. First it was, "The Great American Desert", a vast and tractless waste, a barrier to the gold fields. Unexpectedly and almost overnight it became the potential source of great wealth from livestock raising. And thereon lies the key to the story . . . the major finding of this report . . . at once the most obvious and obscure is range depletion so nearly universal . . .

U.S. Department of Agriculture (1936:3)

The above statement argues that overgrazing was common and destructive throughout the West during the late nineteenth and early twentieth centuries. Whether or not it was as devastating as suggested by the Agriculture Department is unclear. This report was, in part, a promotional tool of the department in its jurisdictional competition with Interior for administration of remaining federal land, an issue addressed in chapter 4. There is evidence, though, that overgrazing was widespread and costly, at least through 1920 when there was major competition between ranchers and homesteaders for the land. This chapter links overgrazing to insecurity of tenure to rangeland due to federal land policy. The chapter details the costs of an open range and the efforts of

13

ranchers to reduce those costs by defining informal property rights to land.

THE PREDICTIONS OF ECONOMIC THEORY REGARDING COMMON PROPERTY CONDITIONS

Common property conditions and the need for defining rights to resources have been discussed by Gordon (1954), Cheung (1970), Alchian and Demsetz (1973), and others, and their arguments can be applied directly to rangeland.

Because of grass and brush cover, the western range was well suited for raising livestock, though its aridity limited other types of argriculture. Irrigation programs and dryland farming techniques, however, were extensively applied. Competition for the land rose as settlement increased in the 1880s. Those holding secure range rights could adjust stocking levels and invest in wells and fences to maximize economic returns. Where property rights could not be established and open-access conditions prevailed, such wealth-increasing decisions were not possible. With many competitors for disputed open range, each individual had incentive to stock the land heavily and harvest it rapidly before others could do so. The result was overgrazing and depletion of land quality as palatable plant species were eliminated and as wind and water more rapidly eroded exposed topsoil. The economic effects of overgrazing were reflected in thin, poor quality cattle and sheep, reduced lambing and calving rates, and high death losses through starvation and disease. Depleted pastures weakened herds, making them vulnerable to extreme weather fluctuations—droughts and severe winters. Open-access conditions kept herd quality low because the returns on individual investment in improved bulls and rams were spread across all herders. Moreover, selection and timing of breeding could not be controlled.

To avoid those conditions ranchers—faced with legal restrictions on formal property rights—often adopted local arrangements to restrict entry and control range use.

INFORMAL PROPERTY RIGHTS ARRANGEMENTS

Customary Range Rights

Table 3-1 outlines available unappropriated land (subject to claiming under the land laws) and the number of cattle and sheep raised in the eleven far western states and territories from 1870 to 1930. While exact figures on the proportion of livestock raised on private and federal land are not available, much of the unappropriated land was pasture, and as late as 1928 the Forest Service estimated that 70 percent of livestock feed came from rangeland (U.S. Department of Agriculture 1928). The growth in animal numbers and decline in available land led to competitive pressure for the range resource.

That pressure is further shown by the pattern of homesteading from 1870 to 1930 listed in table 3-2. Increasingly, homesteaders and ranchers found themselves competing for the same lands, as agricultural settlement pushed into the high plains west of the 100th parallel. Ranchers initially relied on the common law practice of prior appropriation to assign land ownership. Through continual use of an area a stock owner could define his claim:

Table 3-1. Unappropriated Land, Number of Livestock Raised in the Eleven Far Western States

Year	Unappropriated Land	Cattle	Percent of U.S. Total	Sheep	Percent of U.S. Total
1870	708,853	2,780,000	9	7,214,000	20
1880	N.A.	5,453,000	13	16,186,000	36
1890	505,678	9,036,000	15	17,274,000	40
1900	498,302	8,052,000	13	24,803,000	55
1910	333,075	9,183,000	16	28,228,000	60
1920	199,055	12,710,000	18	21,419,000	57
1930	177,966	10,185,000	17	25,045,000	55

Sources: Unappropriated land: U.S. Department of the Interior (annual); livestock numbers: USDA (1937:26-41).

Table 3-2. Homesteading Activity

Year	Total Claims[a]	Total Acreage
1870	33,972	3,754,203
1875	20,668	2,369,782
1880	47,293	6,054,708
1885	50,877	7,415,885
1890	40,244	5,531,678
1895	37,336	5,009,491
1900	61,270	8,478,409
1905	70,344	12,895,571
1910	98,598	18,329,115
1915	62,360	12,439,774
1920	48,532	13,501,100
1925	11,658	3,188,686
1930	13,248	4,920,842

[a]Original Claims and Acreage
Source: U.S. Department of the Interior (annual).

A custom has grown up and become thoroughly established among people of this community that where one stockman has developed water on and taken possession of the range by fully stocking the same that he will not be molested by other stockmen in his possession and enjoyment of such range.[1]

Moreover, the control of water in arid regions served to enforce holdings. Even then, lands which were not heavily stocked were vulnerable to trespass. Accordingly, customary range rights were tenuous, a factor noted by the 1879 Public Lands Commission (1880:245).

The use of continued stocking to define and enforce claims is shown in figure 3-1. In that figure, the value of output per animal and herding costs are measured along the vertical axis; the number of animals is on the horizontal axis. The marginal and average product curves reflect the returns to a rancher from increased stocking. The size of the range determines the location of the curves, and they decline as greater numbers of animals compete for available forage, lowering weight gains. The marginal and average factor cost curves are U-shaped based on empirical evidence of economies of scale in ranching. Studies in both the nineteenth and twentieth centuries revealed clear cost savings from increased size (Peake 1937:86, 247; Youngblood and Cox 1922:234; Parr, Collier, and

Figure 3-1. The Use of Overgrazing as a Means of Defining Rights to Rangeland

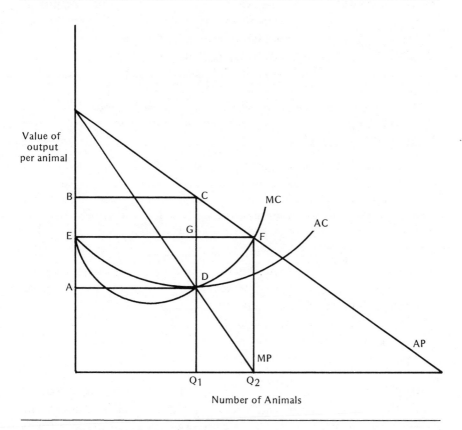

Source: Johnson and Libecap (1980:336).

Klemmendson 1928:55, 59). For example, in 1885 the Bureau of Animal Industry estimated that average herding costs fell from three dollars to one dollar per head as herd size increased from one thousand to three thousand cattle (Taylor 1886:324).

The figure shows that if property rights to the range exist, individual ranchers stock at Q_1, the point where the value of adding one more animal to the range equals added costs. That stocking level maximizes the rental value of the land, ABCD, received by the rancher. Under prevailing open-access conditions, however, ranchers are forced to stock beyond Q_1 to reduce the incentive for entry, attracted by the existence of land rents. Indeed, if all herders have similar costs, the original rancher can increase stocking to Q_2 and make entry less attractive. At Q_2 the average product for the potential entrant equals his average cost (which begins at point F), and the net gains from entry are zero. Thus, following the figure, the typical rancher obtains some degree of exclusivity by increasing herd size, overgrazing, and sacrificing some rents. (This discussion follows that in Johnson and Libecap 1980:334–337.)

The use of overgrazing to define and enforce land claims and the costs involved are illustrated in the following statement by a New Mexico rancher in 1915:

> I can better afford to take the $2,500 loss of stock which I know I will have when the dry years come than to take my stock off my range and try to save some grass which I know I will need in those dry years. I hold my range now only by having my stock on it. If I take my stock off, someone else will take my range, and I can afford to lose the stock better than to lose the range. (Wooten 1915:28)

Enforcement of claims in this way appears to have been increasingly ineffective as settlement advanced, necessitating the need for fencing to more definitely control the range.

Livestock Associations

Another means of defining property rights was through livestock associations, particularly cattlemen's groups, founded throughout the West in the mid-1800s. Herds were pooled to capture economies of scale, and group enforcement of land claims was instituted. For instance, in 1883 Montana ranchers along the Musselshell River claimed some 3,916,800 acres:

> We, the undersigned, stock growers of the above described range, hereby give notice that we consider said range already overstocked; therefore we positively decline allowing any outside parties or any parties locating herds upon this range the use of our corrals, nor will they be permitted to join us in any round-up on said range from and after this date. (Stockslager 1888:5, 6)

Within the boundaries claimed by each association efforts were made to control the stocking of members, since individuals had incentive to overgraze at the expense of others. Generally, the allowable number of animals was based on water ownership (see Peake 1937: 248; Taylor 1886:374; Youngblood and Cox 1922:234; National Livestock Association 1903):

> It will be seen that the ownership of the watering places gives tenure to contiguous range. This fact is recognized by Western cattlemen, and the question as to the number of cattle individual owners are permitted to hold, under regulations of the various local associations, is determined by the questions of water frontage. (Taylor 1886:316)

The cattle of all members grazed together, and annual cooperative roundups were held for branding and marketing. Livestock associations also required each member to supply bulls based on the number of cows in the association herd to insure the spring's calf crop. Moreover, the timing of breeding was controlled so that calves were born in the early spring to increase survival chances and to be ready for fall marketing. These various rules required group negotiation and decision making.

Besides local groups, territorial, state, and national associations were formed to lobby for legislation on brand controls, livestock disease containment, and combating rustling (Peake 1937:104). In some cases, such as Wyoming, those associations became formidable political powers. The Wyoming Stockgrowers Association secured the support of the territorial legislature in its struggle with homesteaders and small ranchers.

While associations were common, there is little available evidence to judge their effectiveness in obtaining more secure tenure to the range. In a recent study Dennen (1976) argued that losses in Wyoming and Montana during the severe winter of 1886-1887 were lower where groups had effectively controlled grazing to conserve winter pastures. He also found that association membership was highly valued and was transferred with ranch property upon sale. That evidence suggests livestock associations were able to increase ranch earnings. Yet, their success also appears to have come early and deteriorated as settlement advanced. Osgood (1929: 186), in his famous study of western ranching, discusses the breakdown of local groups as outside competition for land rose. With uncertainty as to the groups' ability to control entry, the incentive of members to violate internal rules increased. Each attempted to get his share of the grass before the outsiders did. That likely raised the costs of reaching agreement and enforcing association regulations. Increasingly, individual enforcement of claims through fencing emerged as the most viable method of controlling land access and use. Moreover, rising land values in the face of greater demand merited investment in costly fences.[2]

Illegal Fencing of Federal Lands

The extent of private fencing of public land is unknown, but available evidence from historical studies of ranching indicate it was widespread. Tables 3-3 and 3-4 present additional data on fencing. They list enclosed acreage from 1883 to 1919, compiled from Interior records in the National Archives. The data are incomplete, but they show where and when fencing was most common in defining and enforcing claims to federal land. Table 3-3 reveals extensive fencing from 1883 through 1887 as ranchers responded to homestead pressure. The lack of data from 1888 through 1900 reflects reduced antifencing activity by the Interior Department

Table 3-3. Illegal Enclosures in the Eleven Far Western States, 1883-1908 Totals

Year	Total Acreage
1883	2,157,000[a]
1884	2,975,000[a]
1885	1,221,000[b]
1886	6,400,000[b]
1887	8,579,000[b]
1888-1900	Not Reported
1901	2,488,000[b]
1902	3,953,000[b]
1903	2,605,000[b]
1904	1,355,000[b]
1905	363,000[b]
1906	2,000,000[b]
1907	800,000[b]
1908	1,323,000[b]

[a]Colorado only.

[b]Includes Nebraska, North and South Dakota, and Kansas.

Sources: 1883-1887: calculated from Special Agent Reports, Record Group 48, Secretary of the Interior, Central Files, National Archives. 1901-1908: U.S. Department of the Interior (annual).

Table 3-4. Illegal Enclosures by State and Territory, 1909-1919 (in thousands of acres)

Year	NM	AZ	CO	WY	MT	ID	UT	NV	CA	OR	WA	Total[a]
1909	713	35	130	94	31	—	172	14	2	81	9	1,341
1910	303	21	140	47	280	11	68	93	8	20	37	1,162
1911	1,418	23	63	52	12	3	—	—	49	13	5	1,667
1912	58	12	26	—	14	4	—	7	1	15	54	214
1913	368	18	21	11	17	1	—	—	—	5	—	458
1914	127	38	47	37	12	—	—	7	6	6	—	284
1915	122	3	16	—	5	—	—	1	13	—	—	165
1916	68	1	2	—	16	—	—	—	—	—	1	86
1917	26	—	—	11	1	—	—	—	—	1	1	44
1918	3	—	—	4	—	—	—	—	—	—	—	8
1919	3	3	—	7	1	2	1	—	4	—	—	22

[a]Totals may include limited acreage from Nebraska and Dakotas

Source: Special Agent Reports, Record Group 49, Illegal Enclosures, National Archives.

21

Figure 3-2. Enclosure of Alternate Sections of Private and Federal Land

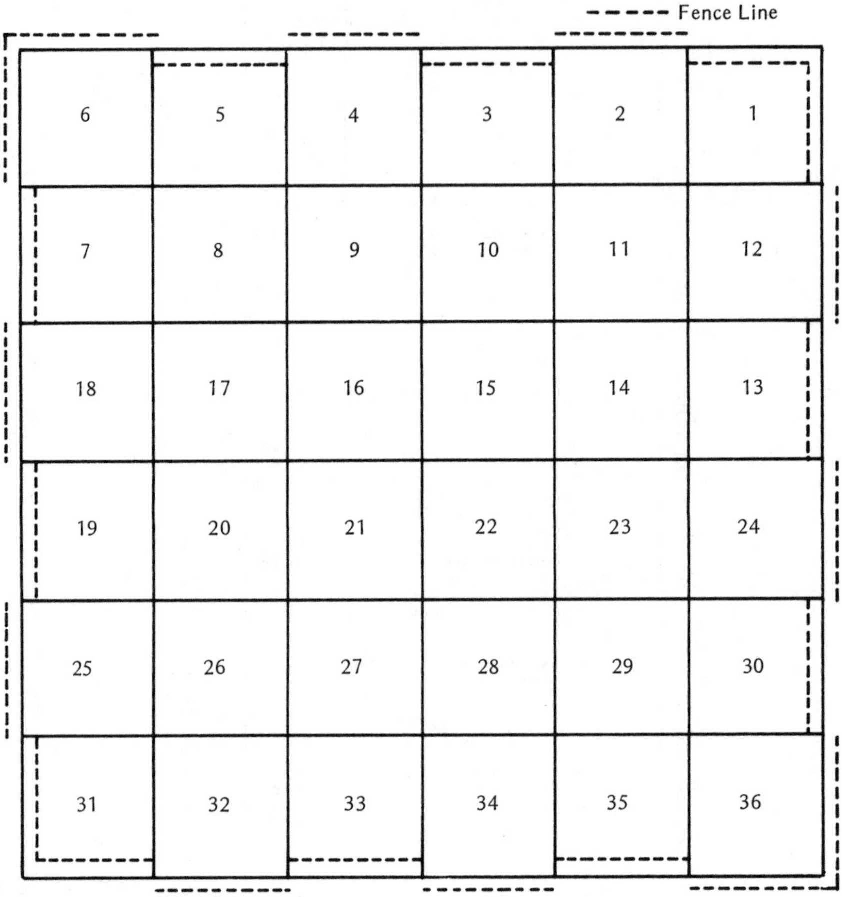

Source: Camfield et al. v. United States, 167 U.S. 518.

rather than fewer enclosures, an issue addressed in the following chapter. Table 3-4 shows that fencing was particularly popular in New Mexico and Colorado. The plains of eastern New Mexico and Colorado were prime grazing areas, and fences were needed to control herds in the absence of natural barriers. Those lands were also inviting to homesteaders—they were flat and close to established farming areas, and large tracts were still available in the early twentieth century. In contrast, grazing lands in Utah and Nevada were more arid, isolated, and mountainous. Rangeland in

New Mexico and Colorado, then, was apt to have been more valuable and subject to more contention for control.

Fences increased ranch values: pastures and water holes could be protected; the drift of livestock could be constrained to prevent straying into areas with poisonous plants, alkali water, or diseased animals;[3] and breeding could be controlled to improve herd quality. Enclosures also raised the collateral value of livestock and land, allowing ranchers to obtain needed credit from bankers and other sources. Their importance was stressed by a New Mexico rancher in response to threats by the Interior Department to remove them. Such action, he argued, "would mean bankruptcy to every stockman now barely getting by with a certain amount of controlled pasture."[4] The types of enclosures used included perimeter fences to define land claims and block access by others, internal fences to establish particular pastures within a ranch, and drift fences which did not enclose an area, but rather controlled the grazing drift of livestock.

Since private enclosure of federal land was illegal, ranchers adopted costly practices to avoid prosecution. Figure 3–2 details the fencing of land in checkerboarded areas common in the West, where privately owned odd sections (former railroad land) were interspersed with federal holdings (even-numbered sections). While fencing of individual 640-acre sections was impractical, careful placing of fence lines only on private land effectively enclosed much larger areas. Fence lines were constructed close enough between adjoining private sections that animals could not pass between them.

THE ECONOMIC COSTS OF OVERGRAZING

The effectiveness of ranchers' extralegal efforts to protect their land claims through continued stocking, livestock associations, and fencing is not clear. Full, common property conditions appear to have been prevented in many areas, particularly through fencing. Tenure, however, was always uncertain given competition from settlers and hostile reaction from the Interior Department. As chapter 4 shows, the department opposed the actions of ranchers and removed their enclosures. Where fences temporarily escaped the surveillance of Interior's special agents, there was continued risk of discovery and prosecution. Hence, U.S. policy kept property rights confused and insecure, weakening access controls and shortening time horizons. The result was overgrazing in many areas.

There are no studies of the trend or aggregate impact of overgrazing on the value of rangeland. After 1900 experiment stations in the Department of Agriculture reported the effects of intensive harvesting on particular pastures. The department repeatedly stressed that uncertain control created pressure for immediate use of rangeland. For example, a 1916 Department of Agriculture study commented:

> The only protection a stockman has is to keep his range eaten to the ground, and the only assurance that he will be able to secure the forage crop any one year is to graze it off before someone else does. (Barnes and Jardine 1916:16)

Overstocking made herds vulnerable to drought, forcing the dumping of animals on the market, a point raised in a 1922 study:

> On an overgrazed range there is never much, if any, reserve feed, so that whenever a drought occurs, the stock must be taken off . . . such forced removals are nearly always undesirable because prices are likely to fall when there is no alternative but to throw large numbers on the market. (Wooten 1922:28)

The impact of depleted pastures on ranch operations is shown in figures 3-3 and 3-4, which detail comparative herd losses and calving rates from 1913 through 1924. The compared areas are the Jornada Range Reserve in southern New Mexico, controlled by the Agriculture Department, and adjacent open-access rangeland. While the reserve was not operated to maximize profits and hence practices may have deviated from those adopted by ranchers under secure tenure, the patterns illustrate the costs of overgrazed rangeland.

A 1925 study of 111 ranches in the Southwest by the U.S. Department of Agriculture provides more exact comparative data for the impact of tenure on production. The study included twenty-eight ranches in far west Texas where 73 percent of the acreage was owned and the rest leased, and eighty-three ranches in southern New Mexico and Arizona where only 8 percent of the land was privately held with the rest open range. Ranch sizes in both areas were similar—an average of 2,305 cattle per ranch in Texas and

Figure 3-3. Mortality as a Percentage of Herd Size on Controlled and Open Range

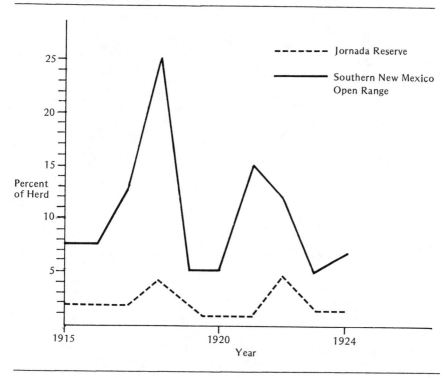

Source: U.S. Department of Agriculture (1924:65).

2,087 in New Mexico and Arizona. Climate and topography were also comparable.

Table 3-5 outlines the performance of ranches in the two areas. The data in the table show the calf crop 47 percent greater for ranches with secure tenure; the death loss 54 percent lower; average cow weight 15 percent greater; and the average value per cow 43 percent higher than for ranches relying on the open range. The researchers argued that the differences in animal quality for the two areas were due to both poorer forage and the lack of incentive for ranchers to invest in improved breeds:

> It is futile for an individual to purchase good quality bulls at high prices for use on the open range when inferior bulls of other operators graze on the same range. (Parr, Collier, and Klemmendson 1928:16)

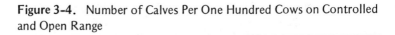

Figure 3-4. Number of Calves Per One Hundred Cows on Controlled and Open Range

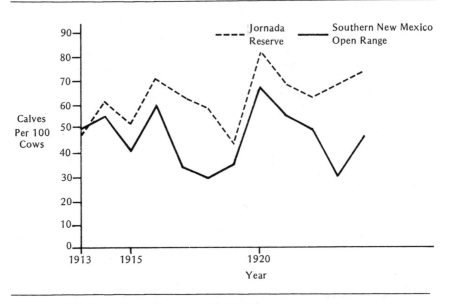

Source: U.S. Department of Agriculture (1924:54).

Ranchers without secure tenure were also reluctant to invest in range improvements; expected returns were apt to be low since any benefits would be spread among all herders. Expenditures per head in wells was $7.30 in west Texas, compared with $2.85 in New Mexico. Investment in fences in the two areas was closer, $2.50 per head compared with $2.16 (ibid.:24).

The high death losses were blamed on poor forage which led to starvation or seriously weakened cattle, vulnerable to disease:

> There is no doubt that the death losses suffered by ranchmen during the dry years were greater than they would have been if the range had not been stocked according to the amount of feed available in good years. (ibid.:43)

Finally, the study emphasized higher labor costs when herds had to be continually monitored because of unprotected pastures. Exact comparisons cannot be made, however, because the researchers did not include family labor input when compiling labor costs.

The implications of the open-access range are clear, and conditions were likely duplicated elsewhere in the West. The figures in the table suggest that secure tenure would have increased the value of the

Table 3-5. Herd Production across Tenure Conditions, 1925

	West *Texas Ranches* with *100 percent* owned or leased land	New Mexico and Arizona ranches with 8 percent owned or leased land
Cow Crop (number per 100 cows)	50%	34%
Cow Death Rates (as percentage of herd)	6.9%	15%
Average Cow Weight	852 lbs.	743 lbs.
Average Calf Weight	380 lbs.	289 lbs.
Average Value of Cattle	$40	$28

Source: Parr, Collier, and Klemmendson (1928): crop and death rates are from table 3, p. 18; weights are from table 14, p. 48; and cattle values are the average of those reported for the opening and closing inventories, table 8, p. 35, and table 9, p. 36.

cattle stock in Arizona and New Mexico, where the study is relevant, by at least 8 percent in 1925.

The 8 percent increase in herd value was calculated as follows: 1943 Interior Department data showed 34 percent of the cattle raised in New Mexico, and 13 percent in Arizona, came from public lands. Those percentages were used to calculate the proportions of the cattle from private and public lands in the two states from the 1925 *Agricultural Census.* The census broke herds into calves, heifers, cows, steers, and bulls. Using the death and calving rates from the table, the hypothetical herd sizes, values, and calf crops were calculated for the two states, assuming secure tenure. Those figures were compared with actual values calculated with the price data from the table. The 8 percent increase understates the difference in value from well-defined property rights because only cow losses were considered, since no data were provided for other herd categories. Moreover, 1925 was a relatively wet year, providing all pastures with better than average grass stands.

Caution, though, is necessary for generalizing beyond the study area. Whether total herd size throughout the West would have expanded or contracted with formal property rights depends upon land quality and prices. Normally, elimination of open-access conditions results in fewer cattle on the range as ranches adjust to longer time horizons. If, however, overgrazing importantly reduced the carrying capacity of the land, formal property rights would lead to greater animal numbers as forage improved. The dynamic effects of overstocking on land quality, however, have not been established, and that limits the conclusions which can be drawn.

Despite the efforts of ranchers, costly overgrazing occurred through the 1920s because property rights to land were not defined and enforced, principally due to the Interior Department and U.S. land policy. The following chapter details the response of the department to the informal efforts of ranchers to exert control over large tracts of land. It also shows the shift in the department's position regarding homesteading in the 1920s. Throughout the discussion, Interior is described not only as a bureaucracy under pressure from Congress and interest groups, but one which enforced laws and sought new ones in its self-interest.

NOTES

1. Sworn statement by William Jones, rancher, Eddy County, New Mexico, 10 April 1917. Record Group 49, Unlawful Enclosure, Box 799, U.S. Archives. Water law is outlined by Trelease (1974).
2. Anderson and Hill (1975) outline efforts to more precisely define property rights as land values rose.
3. Scabies was a particular problem on the open range, spreading rapidly as herds mixed.
4. Letter from R.J. Muir to the U.S. Attorney for New Mexico, 1921. Record Group 49, Unlawful Enclosure, U.S. Archives, Box 859.

BIBLIOGRAPHY

Alchian, Armen, and Harold Demsetz. 1973. "The Property Rights Paradigm." *Journal of Economic History* 13:16–27.

Anderson, Terry L., and P.J. Hill. 1975. "The Evolution of Property Rights: A Study of the American West." *Journal of Law and Economics* 18:163–179.

Barnes, W. C. 1914. "Stock Watering Places in Western Grazing Lands." *Farmers Bulletin* 592:1–27.

_____ . and James T. Jardine. 1916. "Meat Situation in the U.S., Part II, Livestock Production in the Eleven Far Western Range States." *USDA Report* No. 110.

Bentley, H.L. 1898. "Cattle Ranges in the Southwest." U.S. Department of Agriculture *Farmers Bulletin* 72:1-32.

Cheung, Steven N.S. 1970. "The Structure of a Contract and the Theory of a Non-Exclusive Resource." *Journal of Law and Economics* 13 (April):49-70.

Davy, Joseph B. 1902. "Stock Ranges of Northwestern California." U.S. Department of Agriculture *Bulletin* No. 12.

Dennen, R. Taylor. 1976. "Cattlemen's Associations and Property Rights in Land in the American West." *Explorations in Economic History* 13:423-436.

Gordon, H. Scott. 1954. "The Economic Theory of a Common Property Resource: The Fishery." *Journal of Political Economy* 62:124-142.

Griffiths, David. 1901. "Range Improvements in Arizona." U.S. Department of Agriculture, Bureau of Plant Industry *Bulletin* 4.

————. 1902. "Forage Conditions in the Northern Border of the Great Basin." U.S. Department of Agriculture *Bulletin* 15.

————. 1903. "Forage Conditions and Problems in Eastern Washington, Eastern Oregon, Northeastern California, Northwestern Nevada." U.S. Department of Agriculture *Bulletin* 38.

————. 1904. "Range Investigations in Arizona." U.S. Department of Agriculture *Bulletin* 67.

————. 1910. "A Protected Stock Range in Arizona." U.S. Department of Agriculture *Bulletin* 177.

Johnson, Ronald N., and Gary D. Libecap. 1980. "Agency Costs and the Assignment of Property Rights: The Case of Southwestern Indian Reservations." *Southern Economic Journal* 47, no. 2 (October):332-347.

National Livestock Association. Annual. *Annual Reports,* 1900-1930.

Osgood, Ernest Staples. 1929. *The Day of the Cattleman.* Minneapolis: University of Minnesota Press.

Parr, V.V.; G.W. Collier; and G.S. Klemmendson. 1928. "Ranch Organization and Methods of Livestock Production in the Southwest." U.S. Department of Agriculture *Technical Bulletin* 68.

Peake, O.B. 1937. *The Colorado Range Cattle Industry.* Glendale, Co.: Arthur H. Clark Company.

Smith, Jared G. 1899. "Grazing Problems in the Southwest and How to Meet Them." U.S. Department of Agriculture, Division of Agrostology.

Stockslager, S.M. 1888. "Cattle Graziers on Public Lands." *House Executive Document* No. 232, 50th Cong., 1st sess.

Taylor, H.M. 1886. "Importance of the Range Cattle Industry." *Annual Report* of the Bureau of Animal Industry.

————. 1887. "On the Condition of the Range Cattle Industry." *Annual Report* of the Bureau of Animal Industry.

Trelease, Frank J. 1974. *Water Law.* St. Paul, Minn.: West Publishing Company.

U.S. Congress. 1923. "Report of the Public Land Commission." *House Executive Document,* 46th Cong., 2d sess., vol. 22, no. 46, Serial 1923.

U.S. Department of Agriculture. 1924. Jornada Range Reserve. *Annual Report.* Record Group 95, Forest Service, National Archives.

————. 1928. Forest Service. Memo on Range Research, 31 May. Record Group 95, Forest Service, U.S. Archives.

————. 1936. *The Western Range.* 74th Cong., 2d sess. *Senate Document* No. 199.

————. 1937. Bureau of Agricultural Economics. *Livestock on Farms, January 1 By States, Revised Estimates of Numbers, Value per Head, and Total Value, 1867–1919.*

U.S. Department of the Interior, General Land Office. Annual. *Annual Reports.*

Wooten, E.O. 1908. "The Range Problem in New Mexico." U.S. Department of Agriculture *Bulletin* 66.

————. 1915. "Factors Affecting Range Management in New Mexico." U.S. Department of Agriculture *Bulletin* 211.

————. 1922. "The Relation of Land Tenure to the Use of Arid Grazing Lands of the Southwestern States." U.S. Department of Agriculture *Bulletin* 1001.

Youngblood, B., and A.B. Cox. 1922. "An Economic Study of a Typical Ranching Area on the Edwards Plateau of Texas." Texas Agricultural Experiment Station *Bulletin* 297.

4 THE INTERIOR DEPARTMENT AND THE LAND CLAIMS OF RANCHERS

The avowed policy of the government to preserve the public domain for homes for actual settlers has no more implacable and relentless foe than the class that seeks to occupy the public lands for grazing purposes, by maintaining unlawful fences thereon.

U.S. Department of the Interior, *Annual Report of the Secretary* (1902:11).

The theory of bureaucratic behavior outlined in chapter 2 emphasizes the role of discretionary decision making by Interior Department officials to advance their interests. That view is used to analyze the department's opposition to the efforts of ranchers to obtain definite property rights to rangeland. Of particular interest are antifencing policies, actions to block major modification of the homestead laws, and a shift after 1920 from supporting disposal of federal land to advocating bureaucratic management of it.

ANTIFENCING POLICIES

The Interior Department responded quickly to fencing as it began to be commonly used after 1880. The enclosures bound up large areas of land and, accordingly, posed barriers to homesteading.

31

Would-be settlers were frustrated on finding large tracts of desirable land fenced:

> I took up 160 acres of government land . . . It happened to be in a Big Cattle outfit's meadow and when I went to do my Emprovements as required by the laws of the United States of America this same Cattle outfit shut and locked the gates and forbid me to combon my Homestead . . .[1]

Homesteaders complained that the prior appropriation claims of ranchers were tying up the best land. They and their supporters, western businessmen and politicians, called on Interior to break the "monopoly" control of ranchers over the range.[2] Moreover, the Interior Department had to insure that land was available for claiming to maintain long-run budget appropriations for the General Land Office, an agency whose existence depended on continued settlement of western lands.

Until 1885 Interior had no legislative authority to remove the fences, but it actively supported homesteaders' opposition to them. In 1882 and 1883 GLO Commissioner McFarland called for fence removal and the prosecution of ranchers by the Justice Department.[3] In 1883 Secretary of the Interior Teller announced that "this Department will impose no objection to the destruction of these fences by persons who desire to make *bona fide* settlement. . . ."[4] In 1884 both the Senate and the House of Representatives asked Interior to provide them with a summary of the extent of illegal enclosures. The General Land Office responded with a report, *Unauthorized Fencing of Public Lands,* which argued that thousands of acres, in some cases whole counties, were fenced. Commissioner McFarland stated:

> I am satisfied from the information received that the practice of illegally enclosing the public lands is extensive throughout the grazing regions, and that many millions of acres are thus enclosed and are now being so enclosed to the exclusion of stock of all others than the fence owners and to the prevention of settlement and the obstruction of public travel and intercourse. (U.S. Senate 1884:3)

If correct, Commissioner McFarland's statement suggests that fencing was successfully mitigating common property conditions on the high plains. It is important to note, however, that those results were not of concern to the General Land Office, which was interested in advancing agricultural settlement. Antifencing legislation was drawn up and passed on 25 February 1885 (23

Stat. 321) authorizing the Interior Department to investigate and order the removal of enclosures. Whether Interior drafted the legislation is not known, but Secretary Teller and Commissioner McFarland did comment on early drafts and testified for its enactment.[5]

Table 4-1 outlines the enforcement of antifencing legislation through 1934. The inconsistency of enforcement is clearly shown, adding to the general confusion regarding property rights and land claims: when fences were removed the land was placed under open-access conditions; when fences remained, they continued to be vulnerable to federal actions. That uncertainty surely contributed to overstocking.

Strict enforcement of the law during the years 1885-1887 began with President Cleveland's order "that any and every unlawful enclosure of the public lands . . . be immediately removed" (Gates 1968:468). This order and the general fervor behind the legislation to protect homesteaders apparently led GLO Commissioner Sparks to misjudge it as mandate for strict compliance with all land laws. He called on the president to use military force in removing fences,

Table 4-1. Enforcement of 1885 Antifencing Legislation

Year(s)	Enforcement Policy
1885-1887	Strict enforcement under General Land Office Commissioner Sparks
1887-1900	Relaxed policy under Interior Secretary Lamar
1901	President Roosevelt calls for compliance with the law
1904-1914	General Land Office orders removal of fences and prosecution of ranchers
1914	Interior Department agrees to examine each case individually to see if enclosures are reasonable
1916	Interior Department orders delays in prosecution to study need for fences
1917	Fences ordered removed
1917-1918	Enforcement relaxed during World War I
1923	Secretary of the Interior Work calls for compliance
1925-1931	Enforcement delayed
1933-1934	Secretary of the Interior Ickes orders prompt removal of fences

Source: Enforcement policies compiled from Interior Department records, Record Group 48, Office of the Secretary of the Interior, Central Classified Files, U.S. Archives.

and at least in Wyoming the military was used.[6] Sparks went further, however, and broadened the attack to include investigation and prosecution of fraudulent land entries. Had he focused on illegal enclosures, he could have met the demands of the homestead lobby and the needs of the General Land Office to insure the availability to land for claiming. Enclosures were principally used by ranchers and could be removed at lower political cost. Fraud, however, was widespread, used by homesteaders and ranchers to acquire acreage beyond that allowed by the land laws (Gates 1968:479–482). Typically entrymen, often relatives, friends, or employees, were employed to file for additional claims under the pretense of settlement, although they were subsequently consolidated into a single farm or ranch. (The use of fraud to speed the assignment of property rights is outlined by Libecap and Johnson 1978.) To combat fraud Sparks created an investigations division in the General Land Office, increased the number of special agents, and suspended processing land claims from 1885 to 1886 to check their validity. Those actions were costly to homesteaders who wished to acquire additional land; moreover, suspension delayed the assignment of title, reducing the collateral value of all claims. Sparks' actions offended ranchers, homesteaders, and western politicians alike. Under fire, Interior Secretary Lamar revoked the suspension order, replaced Sparks in 1887, and adopted a more reserved posture for the GLO.[7]

Table 3–3 shows that the General Land Office did not renew antifencing actions until 1900 when Theodore Roosevelt became president. The experience of the General Land Office from 1888 to 1900 reveals the limits of bureaucratic discretion. Controversial actions alienating important lobby groups resulted in intensive congressional monitoring, jeopardizing the office's congressional mandate and budget.

After 1900 fencing became a bargaining tool used by the president and the Departments of Agriculture and the Interior to gain the support of the livestock industry for the various land policies they promoted. In 1901 President Roosevelt called for strict enforcement of the antifencing law, and in 1902 GLO Commissioner Hermann charged that enclosures were blocking settlement (Peffer 1951:77). Interior Secretary Hitchcock followed with an order to remove illegal fences on federal lands. That action jeopardized both possessory range rights and the ranches based on them (Gates 1968:487).

In contrast, Gifford Pinchot, of the Department of Agriculture's Forestry Division, offered ranchers the right to maintain fences in the national forests if they supported the transfer of the forests from Interior to Agriculture (American National Livestock Association 1900). The 1905 Public Lands Commission, of which Pinchot was a member, detailed the confused nature of property rights to the range, and a plan attached to the commission's report called for the organization of grazing districts under the jurisdiction of the Department of Agriculture. Roosevelt supported both the transfer of the national forests and the grazing district proposal and backed the offer to allow fencing in the districts. Those efforts were successful in winning the support of the American National Livestock Association for the transfer of the national forests, and in 1905 the forests were placed under the Agriculture Department (American National Livestock Association 1905). Rangeland outside the national forests remained open to claiming, and antifencing activity there continued. A General Land Office circular dated 23 March 1907 ordered special agents to take initiative in prosecuting violations and not to wait for complaints from settlers.

That Interior Department initiative reflects an apparent decline in protests from homesteaders. As homesteading dwindled in the twentieth century, the effect of fences as barriers to entry diminished, while their relative beneficial effects on established farms and ranches increased. An examination of antifencing cases filed during the period 1909–1919, found in Interior Department records in the National Archives, reveals few complaints by settlers. Most cases were initiated by Interior Department agents.[8] Significantly, the files indicate that established homesteaders benefited from the fences constructed by ranchers, since they kept livestock from cropland. Those fences also formed secure partial boundaries for homesteads, and farmers could complete enclosure of their property by attaching new fence lines to existing ones. Nevertheless, as the record subsequently shows, during the 1920s and early 1930s the Interior Department used threats to pressure ranchers to remove their fences from federal land.

Ranchers in the southwestern United States were particularly vulnerable to those threats because of a high incidence of scabies and hoof-and-mouth disease in the area, and the common existence of alkali water, poisonous to livestock. Fences were needed to segregate and quarantine diseased animals and to control the drift of healthy ones from unsafe areas. During World War I antifencing activities were suspended to insure steady supplies of meat—an ironic recognition of the importance of fences for controlling grazing practices and managing herds to increase the value of production. No sustained effort to prosecute ranchers followed until 1923. At that time the Interior and Agriculture Departments were competing for jurisdiction over unreserved rangeland in the West, and rancher political support was important. (By 1923 homesteading was no longer an issue.) Interior Secretary Work used a carrot-and-stick approach to win the backing of stock owners. On the one hand, he initiated renewed enforcement of the 1885 legislation on the open range; on the other, he offered to let fences remain on any lands placed under Interior's control. General support by livestock associations for Interior's proposals was secured, and that may have contributed to delays in fence removal until 1933. Impatient with congressional response to the Interior-supported Taylor Grazing Act and lukewarm rancher support, Interior Secretary Ickes in 1933 again threatened to tear down enclosures on public lands. He asserted that small farmers were being squeezed out and that the 1885 law gave him no option but to order removal.

Both assertions are suspect. In 1933 most of the remaining illegal fencing was in the Southwest, where drought, intense even for that arid region, was driving all but the most efficient operators out of business. Such conditions do not suggest increased demand for land; moreover, Interior Department Solicitor Margold informed Ickes that he had the authority to suspend prosecution of fencing violations.[9] Ickes ignored the opinion and called for prompt destruction of remaining enclosures. As Secretary Work had done ten years earlier, Ickes promised to authorize fencing on any lands subsequently placed under Interior administration.[10]

INTERIOR'S STAND ON LEGISLATION
AFFECTING RANGELAND THROUGH 1920

Until the 1920s the Interior Department opposed the setting aside of land for grazing districts as advocated by the Agriculture Department. That would have reduced the available land for settlement. The principal role of the General Land Office was to survey, validate, and process land claims, and 160 acres had been a basic plot size under the land laws since before the Northwest Ordinance of 1787.

Alloting the vast federal holdings west of the 100th parallel in 160-acre parcels not only insured a supply of farm plots to satisfy homesteaders, but also provided a continuing demand for the bureaucratic services of the GLO. GLO Commissioner Hermann, for example, stated in regard to 1901 grazing legislation:

> It is needless to say that such a bill, if enacted into law, would place the last acre of desirable public land out of the reach of the homeseeker and defeat the purpose of the Government to preserve the public domain for homes for actual settlers. (U.S. Department of the Interior, *Annual Report of the Commissioner* 1902)

The department was concerned with maintaining the viability of homesteading while keeping individual claims as small as possible. While it opposed extension throughout the West of the Kinkaid Act, which allowed 640-acre homesteads in northwest Nebraska, the department backed the 1902 Newlands Reclamation Act to further the homestead potential of arid lands (Hargreaves 1957: 343). That act created a new Interior agency, the Reclamation Service, to construct irrigation systems. Yet, as settlement pressed into dryer regions, 160 acres became a binding constraint, reducing the attractiveness of homesteading and leading to a fall in land office business, as recognized by Commissioner Richards in his 1904 and 1905 *Annual Reports.* Subsequent adjustments in 1909 and 1916, to allow larger homestead claims of 320 and 640 acres respectively, were endorsed by the Interior Department. They competed with bills backed by Agriculture to create grazing districts on federal lands for ranching (Peffer 1951:157). Major increases in homestead claims and acreage followed the more liberal homestead legislation, as figure 4-1 shows. Further, budget appropriations for Interior were raised by $1,172,000 during 1918-1922 to classify land for claiming and to process applications (Gates 1968:518).

THE CHANGE IN INTERIOR LAND POLICIES AFTER 1920

A Shift to Bureaucratic Management

After 1920 the Interior Department halted its advocacy of federal land disposal via the Homestead Act and began to call for central bureaucratic management of the range. It echoed earlier proposals endorsed by the Agriculture Department for the creation of grazing districts on unreserved land and leasing to stock owners, though administration was to be under Interior.

The shift in Interior's position is consistent with the model of self-interest bureaucratic behavior outlined in chapter 2. While as late as 1920 GLO Commissioner Tallman was predicting continued success for stockraising homesteads, total claims as shown in figure 4-1 were definitely down; 640 acres were too few for a viable homestead on remaining arid federal land. The Interior Department

Figure 4-1. Homestead Claims and Acreage, 1885-1933

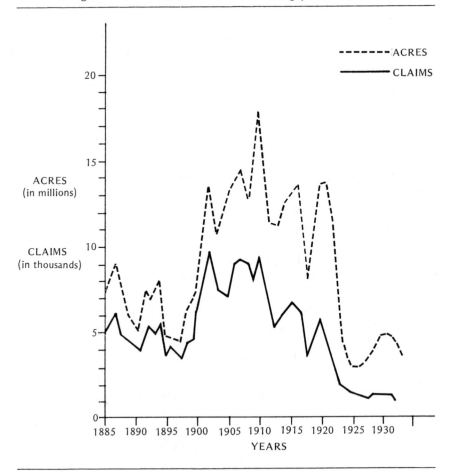

Source: U.S. Department of the Interior, *Annual Reports* of the Commissioner of the General Land Office.

might have called for more generous claims but, significantly, it did not. Instead, it chose to sponsor legislation for grazing districts. There is no record of political pressure on Interior for the turnabout. Rather it appears that after 1920 the secretary and the commissioner viewed central management of federal land as providing a greater source of advancement and growth. There was clearly good reason for that view. Figure 4-2 traces the budget paths for the Forest Service and the General Land Office from 1900 to 1933. While the two agencies had differing mandates, the Forest Service experience must have been illuminating to Interior officials. Under Gifford Pinchot and later chief foresters, the service stressed central, bureaucratic control over natural resouces, and their policies successfully contributed to the rapid growth of the Forest Service. The Forest Service budget passed that of the General Land Office in 1909, only four years after the service was transferred from the Interior Department, and it continued to grow. By contrast, the General Land Office budget leveled and declined. Land disposal no longer provided for longrun expansion of budgets and staff.

Figures 4-3 and 4-4 detail the fall in staffing and fee and commission earnings by General Land Office personnel as claiming subsided. The change in Interior's position and its adoption of the principles of bureaucratic management were illustrated in Interior Secretary Wilbur's call for central planning and rejection of market processes in 1930:

> The adaption of a people to its environment can take place through a thoughtless struggle in the survival of the fittest, or it can be a planned, quiet, and orderly process of human organization. (U.S. Department of the Interior, *Annual Report* of the Secretary 1930:8)

Jurisdictional Struggle for Administrative Control of Federal Rangeland

The change in the Interior Department's land policies aggravated long-standing tension between it and the Department of Agriculture. The two had previously competed for the National Parks Service and the Forest Service (Peffer 1951:178). For instance, in 1919 Interior Secretary Lane, in a letter to President Wilson, and GLO Commission Tallman, in a letter to the Arizona Cattle

Figure 4-2. Annual Appropriations for the Forest Service and the General Land Office (1967 dollars)

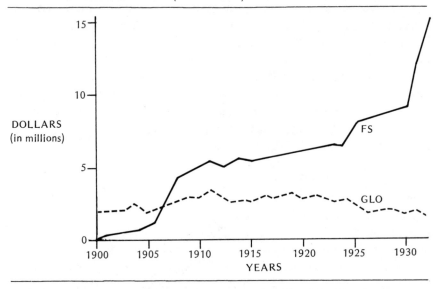

Source: U.S. Department of the Interior, Forest Service, 1899-1916, *Reports of the Chief Forester; U.S. Budgets,* 1920-1933; Canover (1923).

Figure 4-3. Fee and Commission Earnings, General Land Office (1967 dollars)

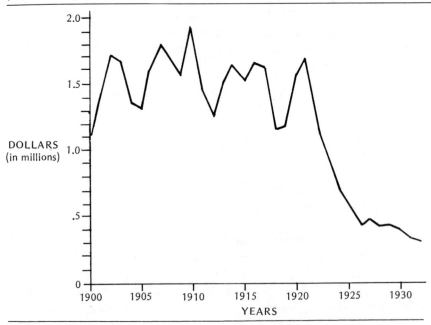

Source: U.S. Department of the Interior, *Annual Reports* of the Commissioner of the General Land Office.

40

Figure 4-4. Staff, General Land Office

Source: U.S. Department of the Interior, *Annual Reports* of the Commissioner of the General Land Office.

Growers Association, called for the return of the Forest Service to Interior.[11] The department's emphasis on bureaucratic management after 1920 placed it in direct contention with Agriculture for jurisdiction over the unappropriated and unassigned rangeland owned by the federal government. More than 170 million acres were potentially involved. In 1921 Interior Secretary Fall offered a bill to assign rangeland to Interior for leasing to livestock owners; Agriculture Secretary Wallace responded with a counter bill. From 1922 through 1934 the Commissioner of the General Land Office lobbied for Interior Department jurisdiction to the range. The Forest Service engaged in counter lobby efforts. For example, the associate forester wrote in 1925 to the assistant secretary of the interior:

> You will understand, of course, that we would naturally view with alarm, and as a matter of self-protection, would be compelled to oppose any measure which would put into effect any system of regulation differing in principle from the system now in effect in the National Forests.[12]

The GLO commissioner responded in 1929 against similar legislation favoring the Forest Service:

> The Department (Interior) has consistently opposed the inclusion of grazing lands, as such, in National Forests as not in harmony with the objects, contemplated by the laws establishing and defining the Federal Forest Reserve Policy.[13]

The interdepartmental dispute may explain why final enactment of leasing legislation did not occur until 1934.

While both departments competed for jurisdiction, they joined in opposing efforts to assign the range to the states or ranchers. That would have placed it beyond their potential control. In 1926 the secretaries of both departments testified against legislation to grant formal grazing rights to ranchers. Interior Secretary Work argued that the bill delegated excessive power to stock owners (U.S. Senate 1926:16). State governments also posed a threat to the two departments by passing local legislation to assign grazing rights in absence of congressional action. State laws were held constitutional by the U.S. Supreme Court in *Omaechevaria* v. *Idaho* (246 U.S. 393). Finally, in 1929 the Garfield Committee appointed by President Hoover suggested remaining federal land be granted to the states, but the suggestion met with only lukewarm western support because valuable mineral rights were to be withheld by the federal government and because federal highway funds would be lost. The latter depended upon the amount of federal land in each western state (U.S. Senate 1932:370).

In 1933 newly appointed Interior Secretary Ickes placed more pressure on ranchers and Congress to enact legislation assigning the range to Interior. Besides enforcing antifencing legislation, Ickes withheld Civilian Conservation Corps (CCC) funds pending congressional action on the Taylor bill. He reminded ranchers that CCC labor could be used to construct range improvements, such as fences, once grazing districts were established. The Taylor Grazing Act was finally passed in 1934, after nearly fourteen years of effort by the Interior Department.

The new mandate for bureaucratic management received from Congress, the Interior Department's relations with ranchers, and the resulting property rights to the range are the subjects of chapter 5.

NOTES

1. Letter from Mr. John Thompson, Viola, Wyoming, to Commissioner, General Land Office, 30 November 1921. Record Group 49, Unlawful Enclosure, National Archives, Box 903.

2. See Peffer (1951:29) for political opposition to claims of ranchers.

3. U.S. Department of the Interior, *Annual Reports* of the Commissioner of the General Land Office (1882–1883); and letter from Commissioner McFarland to Secretary of the Interior Tiller, 27 August 1883. Record Group 48, Office of the Secretary of the Interior, Central Classified Files, U.S. Archives.

4. Interior Department Circular, 19 July 1883. Record Group 48, Office of the Secretary of the Interior, Central Classified Files, U.S. Archives.

5. Intradepartmental views of the antifencing legislation are outlined in a letter from the Commissioner of the General Land Office to Secretary Teller, 26 January 1884. Record Group 48, Office of the Secretary of the Interior, Central Classified Files, U.S. Archives.

6. Letter from Commissioner Sparks to Secretary Lamar, 19 August 1885. Record Group 48, Office of the Secretary of the Interior, Central Classified Files, U.S. Archives; and Gates (1968:474).

7. Gates (1968:475) misses the importance of secure title as collateral by arguing that legitimate settlers weren't hurt by Sparks' actions.

8. Many of the illegal enclosure forms filed by the special agents pointed to the beneficial effects of fencing in protecting homestead farms from straying livestock.

9. Memorandum from Solicitor Margold to Secretary of the Interior Ickes, 11 November 1933. Record Group 48, Office of the Secretary of the Interior, Central Classified Files, U.S. Archives.

10. Letter from Secretary Ickes to Secretary of the American National Livestock Association. Record Group 48, Office of the Secretary of the Interior, Central Classified Files, U.S. Archives.

11. Letters, 11 August 1919, and 16 July 1919. Record Group 48, Office of the Secretary of the Interior, Central Classified Files, U.S. Archives.

12. Letter, 9 January 1925. Record Group 48, Office of the Secretary of the Interior, Central Classified Files, U.S. Archives.

13. Memorandum from Commissioner of the General Land Office to the Secretary of the Interior, 6 June 1929. Record Group 48, Office of the Secretary of the Interior, Central Classified Files, U.S. Archives.

BIBLIOGRAPHY

American National Livestock Association. 1900. *Annual Report of Meetings.*
_____. 1905. *Annual Report of Meetings.*

Canover, Milton. 1923. *The General Land Office.* Institute for Government Research Service, Monographs of the U.S. Government, No. 13. Baltimore: Johns Hopkins University Press.

Dana, Samuel Trask. 1956. *Forest and Range Policy: Its Development in the United States.* New York: McGraw-Hill.

Gates, Paul. 1968. *History of Public Land Law Development.* Washington, D.C.: Public Land Law Review Commission.

Hargreaves, Mary Wilma. 1957. *Dry Farming in the Northern Great Plains, 1900-1925.* Cambridge, Mass.: Harvard University Press.

Libecap, Gary D., and Ronald N. Johnson. 1978. "Property Rights, Nineteenth-Century Federal Timber Policy, and the Conservation Movement." *Journal of Economic History* 39, no. 1:129-142.

Peffer, Louise. 1951. *The Closing of the Public Domain.* Stanford: Stanford University Press.

U.S. Department of the Interior. Annual. *Annual Reports* of the Commissioner of the General Land Office, 1880-1934.

U.S. Department of the Interior. Annual. *Annual Reports* of the Secretary, 1880-1934.

U.S. Senate. 1884. "Unauthorized Fencing of Public Lands." *Executive Document* No. 127. 48th Cong., 1st sess.

U.S. Senate. 1926. "Grazing Facilities on Public Lands." Hearings Before the Commission on Public Lands and Surveys. 69th Cong., 1st sess.

U.S. Senate. 1932. "Granting Remaining Unreserved Public Lands to States." Hearings Before the Committee on Public Lands and Surveys. 72nd Cong., 1st sess.

5 GRAZING PRIVILEGES AND THE TAYLOR GRAZING ACT, 1934-1960
Secure Rights to the Range

Unquestionably the Bureau of Land Management's political weakness in both the Congressional and the departmental level is the most important single reason why the Bureau and its predecessors have never instituted the grazing pattern the Bureau's technicians would like to see.

Calef (1960:259)

The Taylor Grazing Act gave the Interior Department a mandate to manage federal land similar to that received in 1905 by the Agriculture Department and the Forest Service. Yet, at least through 1960, Interior was unable to achieve the same degree of bureaucratic control or to mold a tightly knit organization of technically trained personnel to manage the range.[1] The reason was the department's continuing political weakness, beginning in 1934, which forced it to make broad concessions to ranchers to gain their support. Those concessions diluted the influence of Interior officials over range use. The concessions were of strategic importance because of the sharply differing objectives of ranchers and bureaucrats for administration of rangeland. Established ranchers wanted formal recognition of their informal land holdings at low cost, while Interior Secretary Ickes wanted scientific bureaucratic management with pervasive land use controls. These clashing objectives fueled continuing conflict between stock owners and the department that was to regulate them.

This chapter details the nature of grazing privileges granted ranchers under the Taylor Grazing Act of 1934 and the struggle over bureaucratic controls. The record shows that their political power gave stock owners formal, near proprietary rights to federal lands for nearly thirty years, a contrast to the informal, limited controls existing from 1880 to 1934. After 1934 overgrazing associated with common property situations should have declined and investment increased, and data on land conditions suggest that was the case. Box (1978) reported federal rangeland conditions for 1936, 1966, and 1972. In 1936, 42 percent of the land was classified as fair, good, or excellent; in 1966, 67 percent was so classified, and in 1972, 68 percent. Poor or very poor land declined accordingly.

JURISDICTIONAL DISPUTES AND THE POLITICAL POWER OF RANCHERS

The dispute between the Interior and Agriculture Departments from 1920 to 1941 for administration of federal land was particularly significant for the former. While the massive national forest system of over 170 million acres was assigned to Agriculture, the Interior Department held only the national parks and shrinking Indian reservations which were being dismantled under the congressional policy of assimilation. Accordingly, jurisdiction over the unreserved western range was necessary if the department were to have a long-term, significant role in the management of public lands. Even with the Taylor Grazing Act of 1934, Interior's hold was tenuous because section 13 allowed for transfer to the Forest Service of lands which could "best be administered in connection with existing national forest administration units." In 1935 Secretary Ickes complained that Forest Service officials were campaigning among ranchers for such transfers in violation of a verbal agreement between Grazing Director Carpenter and Forest Service Chief Silcox.[2]

Ickes, however, was also guilty of expansionist plans, lobbying to consolidate all federal lands and conservation efforts, including the national forests and Forest Service, under the Interior Department. Further, he called for an additional 62 million acres to be included under the Taylor Grazing Act to bring the total to 142 million. The new and larger Interior Department was to be renamed the Department of Conservation.

Ickes lobbied for this plans from 1933 to 1941, and in 1939 Congress passed a reorganization bill authorizing President Roosevelt to transfer the Forest Service, but he declined to do so. Interior's efforts were resisted by Secretary of Agriculture Wallace and by bureau chiefs within his department, whose permanent positions were threatened by the proposals (see Ickes 1954:39, 603). The Department of Agriculture responded by issuing a six-hundred-page 1936 study titled *A Report on the Western Range—A Great but Neglected National Resource,* advertising Forest Service successes in range management and pointing to alleged deterioration of lands administered by the Interior Department. Secretary Ickes strongly protested that the *Western Range* was an "attack on a sister department."[3] Despite the intensity of the rivalry, no major land transfers occurred.

The interdepartmental conflict strengthened the position of ranchers. With no experience in range management and little information about land conditions or who occupied the range, Interior depended upon the support of the livestock industry. Sustained resistance to Interior policies by ranchers would have at least delayed, but more likely prevented, the implementation of the Taylor Grazing Act and shifted congressional attention to alternatives—administration by the Forest Service, land grants to western states, or outright sale. Moreover, the political power of ranchers in their home states and among members of Congress was increasing. With the decline of homesteading, ranching reemerged as a viable, permanent economic and political force in western states. No longer was the range livestock industry viewed as a temporary restriction to inevitable, agricultural settlement of western lands. Further, ranchers were well organized in local, state, and national organizations, with the American National Livestock Association the leading national group. Hence, ranchers were influential among western politicians, and, specifically, with those on the Senate and House Committees on Public Lands, committees which reviewed the policies of the Interior Department. The resulting political power of ranchers and the relatively weak position of the Interior Department allowed the former to importantly determine the nature of the grazing privileges granted and the programs adopted under the Taylor Grazing Act, a situation noted by Calef (1960:259) and Clawson (1950:11–14).

GRAZING PRIVILEGES AUTHORIZED BY THE
TAYLOR GRAZING ACT

Section 2 of the Taylor Grazing Act, which was passed on 28 June 1934 (48 Stat. 1269), gave the secretary of the interior broad discretion in creating grazing districts, in establishing rules and regulations, in making cooperative agreements with ranchers and "to do any and all things necessary to accomplish the purposes of this Act . . . " Section 3 authorized the secretary to issue grazing permits for up to ten years to stock owners upon annual payment of "reasonable fees in each case to be fixed or determined from time to time." Secretarial discretion over the permits was constrained by two important provisions: one ordered that preference be given to "land owners engaged in the livestock business" residing in or near each grazing district, "to bona fide occupants or settlers, or owners of water or water rights." The ordering of the priorities, however, was left open. The second provision, added by Nevada Senator McCarran, granted ranchers important security of tenure:

> no permittee complying with the rules and regulations laid down by the Secretary of the Interior shall be denied the renewal of such permit, if such denial will impair the value of the grazing unit of the permittee, when such unit is pledged as security for any bona fide loan.

The secretary was to set the number of animals which could be grazed by each permit holder and the seasons when the range could be used, both of which could be adjusted to his option. Finally, the section asserted ultimate federal control by stating that "the creation of a grazing district or the issuance of a permit pursuant to the provisions of this Act shall not create any right, title, interest, or estate in or to the lands." The permit, then, granted the right to graze, but not property rights to the land. As the analysis subsequently shows, without secure rights to the resource, inefficient land use practices could continue.

Section 9 contained an equally important provision requiring that the secretary cooperate with local livestock associations, state officials, and state conservation agencies in drawing up rules and regulations for the grazing districts. Section 10 provided that the income received from grazing fees be divided as follows: 25 percent to the federal treasury, 25 percent to a range improvement fund, and 50 percent to state legislatures for the counties containing grazing districts.

To make Interior jurisdiction attractive to ranchers, Secretary Ickes offered them broad authority in the assignment of grazing privileges, and in setting carrying capacity and stocking levels. He also appointed a Colorado rancher, Farrington Carpenter, as head of the Grazing Division. Additionally, no grazing fee was to be charged the first year, and Ickes agreed that subsequent fees would be calculated on a cost-of-administration basis rather than forage value. The latter formula had resulted in increased user charges on Forest Service lands. When grazing fees were first levied in 1936, they were five cents per cow per month on Interior lands, while Forest Service rates were thirteen cents (see table 5-2). Ickes promised to keep administration costs low, offering in testimony before Congress to administer the lands for $150,000 in 1935 as compared to the Forest Service estimate of $1.5–$2 million (Gates 1968:611). Finally, in 1935, the first year of the Taylor Act, temporary grazing licenses were issued to all applicants on an annual basis, pending the evaluation of individual claims and determination of range carrying capacity.

These concessions were part of what Grazing Director Carpenter called the developmental phase of Interior's program, reminding Ickes of the need for rancher support: "Their intelligent cooperation is the greatest asset available to the ultimate success of your program."[4] Carpenter called for the election of advisory boards of ranchers in his first administrative order; only ranchers qualified to use Taylor lands were eligible to vote. The local advisory boards importantly determined the assignment of the initial grazing permits. They documented the informal claims of ranchers for federal land, verified base property requirements, set individual stocking levels based on their estimates of the carrying capacity of the range, and suggested seasons of use. The recommendations of the advisory board were almost always followed.[5]

The criteria for the assignment of grazing privileges gave highest priority to applicants who owned land and held water rights and who had used federal rangeland during the period 1929-1934. The commensurate land and water requirement was to insure that alternative pastures were available for livestock when federal land was withdrawn from grazing to rest and reseed. The requirement clearly gave preference to those who owned land. Second priority was given to those who used federal land during the base period but did not have the required commensurate land, and third priority went to those who satisfied the ownership criteria but who did not have a history of prior use.

Carpenter called for a meeting of the elected advisory board members in Salt Lake City in 1935 to discuss the priority scheme and the proposed grazing fees. The grazing advisors voted to reverse the second and third priorities to strengthen the land ownership requirement, regardless of prior use. The intent was apparently to prevent entry by stock owners, particularly "nomadic sheepmen," who depended on federal land for forage and had little or no land of their own (Calef 1960:57). In 1935, 14,653 grazing licenses were issued in thirty grazing districts under the Taylor Grazing Act for 1.5 million cattle and over 6 million sheep.[6]

Standard discussions of the Taylor Grazing Act assert that the priority scheme eliminated small ranchers (Calef 1960:50; Gates 1968:495-527; Foss 1960:69, 183-186; Voigt 1976:253; and Clawson 1950:114). The assertion that the Taylor Act redistributed rangeland cannot be tested, though, without knowledge of the distribution of land holdings prior to 1934. Unfortunately, there is limited evidence to thoroughly examine the issue. Table 5-1 provides a breakdown of the licenses issued by the Interior Department to ranchers by size category and, hence, shows the nature of the distribution after the Taylor Act was passed. Notice that individual permittees received licenses to run a given number of animals. The land area assigned (an allotment) depended on the number of animals to be grazed and was generally the area historically used by the rancher. In most cases, then, licenses formalized past, informal grazing patterns.

The table reveals that the number of licenses was skewed toward small operators for both cattle and sheep, though in terms of the number of livestock, the shares were relatively evenly divided across ranch sizes for cattle and somewhat more skewed toward larger operators for sheep. There is no evidence that small ranchers were routinely pushed out in the assignment of grazing privileges by the local advisory boards, dominated by larger operators. It is unlikely that there were many very small successful ranchers prior to 1934, in any case, since economies of scale in ranching pointed to consolidation of operations. Studies in the Southwest, for example, revealed a sharp drop in average costs as ranch size expanded up

Table 5-1. The Distribution of Grazing Licenses on Interior
Department Lands in 1938

	Number of licenses	Percent of total licenses	Percent of total livestock
Cattle			
50 or less	4622	48.0	9.1
50-150	2834	29.4	17.8
150-300	1225	12.7	17.9
300-600	617	6.4	21.4
600-1500	277	2.9	16.8
over 1500	64	0.6	17.0
Sheep			
1-500	2579	44.8	6.5
500-1500	1585	27.6	20.8
1500-3000	996	17.3	27.6
over 3000	594	10.3	45.1

Source: Memo to Secretary of the Interior Ickes, "Classification of Licenses by Number of Livestock Owned," 24 March 1938. Record Group 48, Interior Department Central Files, Office of the Secretary of the Interior, U.S. Archives.

to eight hundred cattle. Similar size economies existed for sheep ranches.[7] The base period 1929-1934, considered for historical use in the assignment of licenses, was one of severe drought which caused the failure of less efficient ranches. Given these pressures, it is surprising that there were as many small permittees as table 5-1 indicates.

The incidence of disputes over assigned allotments also provides insight for the redistribution question. Widespread controversy regarding the implementation of the Taylor Grazing Act would indicate that existing informal practices and allocations were being rejected. Yet, the total number of serious disputes is small relative to the number of licenses issued. Minor complaints over stocking numbers, allotment areas and so forth were heard by local advisory boards and could be formally appealed to the district grazier, the local Interior Department official. Between 1935 and 1939 there were 2,258 formal appeals, (U.S. Department of the Interior, *Grazing Bulletin* 2, no. 4 [1939]:31), most involving the commensurate land requirement.[8] Those ranchers who did not have sufficient private land and water had their stocking requests cut by the advisory boards. Unresolved, serious issues could be taken to the secretary of the interior. Certainly, any denials of access to federal land by existing ranchers as part of a redistribution scheme would have been appealed to the secretary. From a total of 15,000 licenses, there were six appeals to the secretary in 1935, fifteen in 1936, fifty-nine in 1937, and forty in 1938.[9]

The Taylor Grazing Act authorized ten-year, renewable permits once determination of carrying capacity by the Interior Department was completed. Until that time, annual licenses were issued based on advisory board estimates of range conditions. Despite the attractiveness of the longer-term permits, ranchers did not push for them because of the required official carrying capacity calculation. Experience with the Forest Service taught that the official statistics were generally below those set by advisory boards and led to reductions in authorized stocking. Hence, ranchers preferred annual licenses where authorized animal numbers were determined by advisory boards; the licenses were secure, since section 3 of the Taylor Act required they be renewed if they were collateral for loans, and available evidence indicates that licenses were routinely renewed. The lack of rancher support for data collection and calculation of official carrying capacity delayed the process of assigning ten-year permits. As late as 1940 none had been issued: indeed, the process of assigning permits (called adjudication) was not completed until 1967. (Clawson 1971:85, and Foss 1960:66 claimed that low fee income slowed the process.)

INSTITUTIONAL ASPECTS OF THE INTERIOR DEPARTMENT–RANCHER CONFLICT FOR CONTROL OF THE RANGE

Staffing

The Taylor Grazing Act granted the secretary of the interior broad discretion in creating an administrative structure to manage federal rangeland. Given Secretary Ickes' admiration of the Forest Service and his advocacy of scientific management, he would likely have used that discretion to build a staff of technically trained bureaucrats for the Grazing Service. Stock owners, wary of the latitude allowed the secretary and fearful of an unfriendly Grazing Service, blocked Ickes' efforts with a 1936 amendment to the Taylor Act.

Section 17 was added, requiring that all senior officials—the director of grazing, assistant director, and all district graziers—"be bona fide citizens or residents for one year immediately preceeding their appointment, of the State or one of the States in which they are to serve." Moreover, the amendment required that the Civil Service take into account "practical and range experience" in hiring all personnel. The amendment made it probable that those in the Grazing Service setting policy and those in the field implementing it would be sympathetic to the needs of ranchers. Additionally, the practical experience requirement tended to limit the potentially disruptive scientific management of livestock operations. Individuals with ranching backgrounds were less inclined to adopt abstract, biological range management concepts. Those concepts, discussed in chapter 6, called for sharply different stocking practices than commonly followed by ranchers responding to market conditions. Stock owners successfully influenced the makeup of Interior's range staff from 1936 through 1960. During that time relations at the field level were relatively cordial and the department's actions benign.

Advisory Boards

While advisory boards were established in 1935 by Grazing Director Carpenter to temporarily obtain the cooperation of ranchers in administering the Taylor Grazing Act, the boards quickly became more than advisory bodies. By 1936 they were estimating grazing capacity, setting stocking levels, ruling on license applications, arbitrating disputes, and helping to determine seasons of use for pastures. Their influence over almost every aspect of range management made them essential institutions for advancing the interests of ranchers and for restricting bureaucratic authority. Interior Secretary Ickes was concerned as early as 1935 that the growing authority of the boards would jeopardize the building of a strong regulatory body within Interior. In October 1935 he reprimanded Grazing Director Carpenter for encouraging the boards to be administrative bodies rather than relying on Interior officials. Ickes argued that Carpenter's dependence on the advisory boards was preventing the development of an adequate range conservation program.[10] In January 1936 Ickes reminded the advisory board members at a meeting in Salt Lake City that they had no administrative function but were advisors only. Meanwhile, western legislatures, aware of the boards' influence, attempted to expand the boards' power by giving them authority over the expenditure of state funds received from grazing fees (50 percent of total fee receipts). Secretary Ickes fought the efforts of state governments and was critical of Director Carpenter for not opposing the legislation:

> Here again is a move on your part which might have the effect of dispossessing the Department of the Interior and the United States Government so far as public lands are concerned . . . This Department is not in favor of such legislation as you refer to; it would be quite a different thing if the States decided to forego their share of the fees and leave its administration to the Department of the Interior.[11]

Ickes unsuccessfully lobbied western politicians against granting the boards expenditure authority.[12] In October 1937 the Interior Department solicitor ruled that the state legislation was legal, that advisory boards could receive state money and allocate it as they saw fit; yet the opinion was delayed and not relayed by Secretary Ickes to the field until nearly two years later in 1939.[13]

Director Carpenter resigned in 1938 and was replaced by R. H. Rutledge, an eighteen-year career Forest Service official more in step with efforts to implement bureaucratic management of the range. Rutledge moved to strengthen the department's authority over federal land. He abolished the Salt Lake City field headquarters which had been set up by Carpenter for liaison with western livestock interests and reorganized the Grazing Divisions, consolidating authority in Washington, D.C. He called for increased staffing and central bureaucratic management of land use following the Forest Service example.[14]

Ickes' hostility and Rutledge's efforts at centralizing authority threatened both the temporary advisory boards and the grazing privileges held by ranchers. Accordingly, livestock organizations moved to strengthen their position by making the advisory boards permanent and limiting the secretary's discretion over them. Beginning in 1937 resolutions were passed by the American National Livestock Association, the Arizona Cattle Growers Association, and other groups to obtain legal recognition and protection for the boards. In 1939 Nevada Senator McCarran successfully amended the Taylor Grazing Act, adding section 18 to require that the secretary consult with district advisory boards of five to twelve members, which were to meet at least once a year:

> In order that the Secretary of the Interior may have the benefit of the fullest information and advice concerning physical, economic, and other local conditions in the several grazing districts, there shall be an advisory board of local stockmen in each district . . .

Moreover, the amendment gave congressional backing for the advisory board's role in the assignment of grazing licenses and the management of grazing districts:

> Each board shall offer advice and make a recommendation on each application for such a grazing permit within its district. . . . Each board shall further offer advice or make recommendations concerning rules and regulations for the administration of this Act, and establishment of grazing districts, and the modification of the boundaries thereof, the seasons of use and carrying capacity of the range, and any other matters affecting the administration of this Act within the district.

What had been previously left to the secretary was now required by law. Through section 18, the existence and role of the advisory boards in defining and protecting grazing rights were guaranteed.

In 1939 six hundred ranchers were members of local district boards (U.S. Department of the Interior, *Grazing Bulletin* 2, no. 4 [1939]:3). State advisory boards and a national board called the National Advisory Board Council were created in 1940 to make recommendations and lobby on issues of more general impact on the livestock industry. They received similar legislative endorsement with a 1949 amendment to the Taylor Act. The advisory boards remained potent factors in influencing range administration until 1978.

Grazing Fees

Besides advisory boards, ranchers and Interior officials struggled over the level of grazing fees. In 1934, when rancher support was crucial for passing and implementing the Taylor Grazing Act, Secretary Ickes downplayed the significance of user charges: no fee was levied in 1935 and subsequent fees were to be based on administrative costs, not forage value. The 1936 fee was five cents per cow per month, and table 5-2 shows that Interior charges were

Table 5-2. Forest Service and Grazing Service Fees[a]

Year	Forest Service	Grazing Service (after 1946 Bureau of Land Management)
1936	.13	.05
1937	.13	.05
1938	.15	.05
1939	.13	.05
1940	.15	.05
1941	.16	.05
1942	.19	.05
1943	.23	.05
1944	.26	.05
1945	.25	.05
1946	.27	.05
1947	.31	.08
1948	.40	.08
1949	.49	.08
1950	.42	.08

[a]Per cow per month in actual dollars.

Source: Study of Fees for Grazing Livestock on Federal Lands, a report from the Secretary of Agriculture and the Secretary of the Interior (Washington, D.C., 1977), pp. 2-4, 2-5.

kept well below those of the Forest Service. Indeed, increases in user fees by the Forest Service in the 1920s had been a major source of contention between the agency and ranchers and likely accounted for the lack of rancher support for Forest Service jurisdiction over federal rangeland.

In 1940 Secretary Ickes called for higher grazing fees to reflect the increased value of the range (U.S. Department of the Interior, Annual Report 1940:336). Since any fee increase would be resisted by livestock groups, Ickes' call reflected the greater security of Interior's jurisdiction over the range and the need to raise revenue to finance an expansion of bureaucratic management. Administrative costs had risen to nearly $2.7 million by 1940 while fee income was over $3 million. Yet, 50 percent of that was returned to the states, and 25 percent was earmarked for range improvements, leaving only 25 percent or $750,000 for the Treasury (Peffer 1951: 261).

The shortfall brought criticism from the Bureau of the Budget that charges were too low.[15] Finally, fees were tied with the range tenure issue, which repeatedly resurfaced after 1934. There was concern within the department that low user fees were creating among ranchers a sense of proprietary rights to federal land.[16] The Taylor Act essentially required that licenses and permits be automatically renewed and transferable, and the gap between the levied grazing fee and the market value of the forage was capitalized in the price of ranches when they were sold. That gave the grazing privileges held by ranchers the flavor of a private property right.[17]

The Nevada legislature was particularly hostile to proposed fee increases, and Nevada Senator McCarran led the opposition to them in Congress. There were a number of probable reasons for the strength of Nevada's opposition to Interior policies. One was that the state contained more federal land than any other and was therefore more vulnerable to bureaucratic actions. It was also probable that Nevada ranchers were least dependent upon the regulatory power of the Interior Department to control entry and land use. Since the 1920s the state legislature had supported the informal holdings of established livestock owners through statutes recognizing and enforcing their claims.[18] The state also had the largest permittees and license holders both in terms of acreage and number of animals. Average acreage per permit or license in the late 1930s was 27,022 acres in Nevada, compared with 16,131 acres in Arizona, the next largest, or Montana the lowest at 1,636 acres. In addition Nevada ranchers had an average of 364 cattle per license while the other western states had an average of 180.[19]

In May 1941 the U.S. Senate passed Resolution 241 authorizing Nevada Senator McCarran, of the Senate Committee on Public Lands, to investigate the policies of the Grazing Service. The hearings lasted until 1947, and they were severely critical of proposed fee increases and expanded bureaucratic control of the range. Senator McCarran unsuccessfully tried to amend the Taylor Act to make charges subject to approval of the local advisory boards (Foss 1960:179). Because of World War II, the fee issue was tabled at the suggestion of the National Advisory Board Council. The limited income received by the Interior Department, though, imposed an important constraint on its ability to adopt new range programs.

In 1944 the question of fees reappeared. Clarence Forsling of the Forest Service replaced R. H. Rutledge as Director of the Grazing Service, and he called for trebling of fees to fifteen cents and tying them to forage value, not administrative costs (Foss 1960: 181). Though unsuccessful in 1944, Secretary Ickes and Director Forsling lobbied for higher levies through 1946.[20] By that year fee income was critical not only to expand the Grazing Service's budget, but to protect its current appropriations. Both the Bureau of the Budget and the House Appropriations Committee pressured the Interior Department to raise revenue as a condition for favorable budgetary actions (Foss 1960:180–184).[21] Livestock groups united in opposition, forming the Joint Livestock Committee on Public Lands, made up of the National Woolgrowers Association, the American National Livestock Association, and the National Advisory Board Council. The Joint Committee lobbied against fee increases and for cuts in appropriations to the Grazing Service. A compromise was finally agreed to in late 1946, raising levies to eight cents per cow per month rather than fifteen cents as proposed by Secretary Ickes. The new grazing fee accepted by ranchers also increased the Treasury's income share to approximately 56 percent (Peffer 1951:272). The probable reason for that change was to raise the revenue received by the government to reduce pressure from the House Appropriations Committee for further user charges. The new fee, however, did not satisfy the Appropriations Committee, which retaliated by cutting the Grazing Service's budget by over half and forcing a major cut in staffing. Congressman Johnson, chairman of the committee, stated:

> . . . a certain former Secretary of the Interior appeared before . . . Congress and assured us that it could operate on $150,000 a year and that it would be self-supporting. . . . But what did the Grazing Service do? They went out and practically turned it over to the big cowmen and the big sheepmen of the West . . . we gave them $425,000, the amount they collected . . . and we said to the Grazing Service: "Live up to your contract; live within your revenue." and by the eternals they are going to do it whether they like it or not. (Foss 1960:186)

Reorganization of the Grazing Service followed, and it was combined with the General Land Office to form the Bureau of Land Management.

Table 5-3 outlines the growth in appropriations and staffing of the service through 1945 and the impact of the successful re-

Table 5-3. Annual Appropriations and Staff for the Grazing Division
of the Interior Department, 1934-1947

Year	Appropriation[a]	Staff
1935	$ 150,000	—
1936	250,000	36
1937	650,000	90
1938	800,000	109
1939	900,000	147
1940	1,000,000	250
1941	1,791,298	246
1942	1,876,000	298
1943	2,603,854	295
1944	3,239,159	417
1945	2,309,240	353
1946	1,754,420	250
1947	802,500	86

[a]actual dollars

Source: Appropriations: 1935-1946, Peffer (1951); 1947-1950, Gates (1968). The figures presented by Peffer from 1941-1946 are larger than those given for the Grazing Service in the *U.S. Budget.* They, however, correspond to figures used by Gates and are used here. CCC allocations are not included. Staff data are from the following sources: 1936, 1947, Gates (1968); 1932, Calef (1960); 1940-42, Foss (1960); 1946, Peffer (1951); 1938, 1939, 1941, 1943, 1944, 1945, from *U.S. Budget.* Budget staff data tend to be slightly larger than those given in the other sources. After 1947 the Grazing Division was merged with the General Land Office, and budget data are no longer comparable.

sistance of ranchers, resulting in a fall in appropriations and staffing in 1946 and 1947. The table also reveals the constraints placed on the Grazing Service by the need to accomodate livestock owners. For thirteen years the staff remained under five hundred and the budget under $4 million. In contrast the Forest Service, with similar acreage to administer though with differing functions, had a staff of over 3,700 in 1941 and a budget for general expenses and salaries of $14.5 million. (See *U.S. Budget* [1943] for actual 1941 appropriations for the Forest Service.)

Despite its sharply reduced budget and staff, ranchers did not want the Grazing Service dismantled, bringing a possible return to open-range conditions. Moreover, grazing licenses with minimal fees and bureaucratic regulation were likely preferable to private property rights. There was every indication that stock owners could continue to control Interior policies; private property rights would have involved an auctioning of western lands, since the political climate of the late 1940s ruled out a mere transfer of title to existing users. Not only would auctions have brought a wealth loss to ranchers by forcing them to buy rangeland, but outcomes were uncertain. Finally, private lands were subject to local property taxes, which were substantial in some areas. While subsequent events were to prove that ranchers misjudged their ability to limit bureaucratic control, in 1947 they acted to prevent the collapse of Interior's grazing program from insufficient funding. Advisory boards contributed $150,000 from their share of grazing receipts (the shares Ickes had earlier attempted to block) to pay the salaries of local Grazing Service employees (Peffer 1951:274). Now, as sources of income, the advisory boards had greater authority than before over the district officials.

The success of stock owners in "capturing" the Grazing Service is probably the reason for their lukewarm support of efforts to sell federal rangeland from 1946 to 1948 (Peffer 1951:287). By successfully holding down the level of user fees ranchers not only demonstrated their political clout, they also limited the bureaucratic functions of the service. Official determination of grazing capacity which might have led to stocking cuts was delayed due to a shortage of funds, and federally financed range improvements were curtailed (Peffer 1951:277). Despite the attractiveness of subsidized improvements, there were reasons for ranchers to oppose them. Investments made by the Interior Department strengthened the government's claim to the land, while private expenditures had an opposite effect. That effect was recognized by the solicitor in 1945 when he rejected an application for private wells on federal land for watering livestock:

> It is inevitable . . . that a permittee who expends his own money to improve the range pursuant to such an agreement will feel that the Government is under some moral or equitable obligation to renew the permit or accord him a preference right of one kind or another.[22]

A COMPLIANT BUREAU AND SECURE TENURE TO THE RANGE

The Bureau of Land Management (BLM) was organized in 1947 from two decimated agencies: the General Land Office, the old land disposal agency, and the Grazing Service, which had just received sharp budget and staffing cuts. Livestock groups which forced the reorganization kept up pressure on the BLM to insure continuation of the administrative structure based on the advisory boards and the secure grazing privileges granted ranchers. F. W. Johnson, the first director named by Secretary Krug (who replaced Ickes in 1946), was opposed to the National Advisory Board Council and the Joint Livestock Committee on Public Lands. He agreed to keep grazing fees low and to tie them to administrative costs as recommended by the National Advisory Board Council.[23] Nevertheless, he was replaced in 1948 by Marion Clawson. The BLM under Clawson was essentially a custodial agency with limited manpower and funding. Clawson commented in 1950 that "it is unlikely if today any public land policy could be adopted which was unitedly and strongly opposed by the range livestock industry" (Gates 1968:625). Through 1960 the Bureau of Land Management worked closely with the district advisory boards in managing federal rangeland and in safeguarding the grazing privileges held by ranchers. In his study of grazing districts in Wyoming during that period, Wesley Calef (1960) noted that stocking cuts were done only with the approval of the advisory boards and nearly unanimous agreement of permittees. In a similar study in Oregon at the same time, Phillip Foss (1960) commented:

> Boards appear to be the dominant rule-making (policy-formulating) body in the federal grazing service. The boards also are involved in management details and in fact, no part of the administration appears to be barred from their surveillance. (Foss 1960:135)

By 1960 ranchers had successfully expanded the authority granted them over federal rangeland when the Taylor Grazing Act passed. The following chapter shows those conditions were not to survive intensive efforts by the BLM to expand bureaucratic control over the range.

NOTES

1. Pinchot (1947) discussed his philosophy for the Forest Service and the need for scientific management by an elite, technically trained organization.
2. Letter from Secretary Ickes to Rex Tugwell, 23 April 1935. Record Group 48, Interior Central Files, Office of the Secretary, U.S. Archives.

3. Letter from Secretary Ickes to Secretary Wallace, 14 July 1936. Record Group 48, Interior Central Files, Office of the Secretary, U.S. Archives.

4. Letter from Director Carpenter to Secretary Ickes, 8 November 1935. Record Group 48, Interior Central Files, Office of the Secretary, U.S. Archives.

5. Memo from First Assistant Secretary Walters, 10 March 1937, stated that the recommendation of advisory boards was generally followed. That also is consistent with studies of the administration of federal land by Calef (1960) and Foss (1960). See Walters memo, Record Group 48, Interior Department Central Files, Office of the Secretary, U.S. Archives.

6. "Grazing Licenses Issued by the Division of Grazing, U.S. Department of the Interior, 1935." Record Group 48, Interior Central Files, Office of the Secretary, U.S. Archives.

7. Economies of scale in western ranching are addressed by Martin (1963, 1978); Goodsell, Gray, and Belfield (1974); and Parr, Collier, and Klemmendson (1928).

8. Complaints in Interior Department files, Record Group 48, U.S. Archives, center on stocking cuts and the issue of commensurate property. Some ranchers protested the requirement to have sufficient private land to graze livestock during seasons when federal lands were unavailable. They argued that during such times they could buy alternate feed. Interior did not agree and stocking cuts were imposed in those cases. See, for example, the resolution of the Harvey County Stockmen's Association, 23 October 1937.

9. Memo from Solicitor to Secretary Ickes, 27 June 1938, and *Grazing Bulletin* 2, no. 4 (1939). Record Group 48, Interior Central Files, Office of the Secretary, U.S. Archives.

10. Letter from Secretary Ickes to Director Carpenter, 31 October 1935. Record Group 48, Interior Central Files, Office of the Secretary, U.S. Archives.

11. Letter from Secretary Ickes to Director Carpenter, 8 March 1937. Record Group 48, Interior Central Files, Office of the Secretary, U.S. Archives.

12. For example, Ickes sent letters to Representative Murdock of Utah (12 March 1937) and a telegram to Senator Pope of Idaho (16 July 1938) arguing that the boards had no legal status and should not receive state fee revenues. Record Group 48, Interior Department Central Files, Office of the Secretary, U.S. Archives.

13. Department Circular W-123, 11 August 1939. Record Group 48, Interior Central Files, Office of the Secretary, U.S. Archives.

14. Memo from Director Rutledge to Secretary Ickes, 14 April 1939. Record Group 48, Interior Central Files, Office of the Secretary, U.S. Archives.

15. Letter from Acting Director Cay to Secretary Ickes, 10 September 1942. Record Group 48, Interior Central Files, Office of the Secretary, U.S. Archives.

16. Letter from Secretary Ickes to Assistant Secretary Chapman, 24 September 1943. Record Group 48, Interior Central Files, Office of the Secretary, U.S. Archives.

17. Gardner (1962) discusses the capitalization of grazing permit values.

18. The Stock Watering Act passed by the Nevada legislature restricted access to the range to those who held water rights.

19. Report of the Grazing Division, Department of the Interior, 1937. Record Group 48, Interior Department Central Files, Office of the Secretary, U.S. Archives.

20. Secretary Ickes sent letters to western senators lobbying for fee increases. Copies are on file in Record Group 48, Interior Central Files, Office of the Secretary, U.S. Archives.

21. Also see Secretary Ickes letter to Bureau of the Budget Director H. Smith, 31 January 1945. Record Group 48, Interior Central Files, Office of the Secretary, U.S. Archives.

22. Memo from Solicitor to Assistant Secretary of the Interior, 17 August 1945. Record Group 48, Interior Central Files, Office of the Secretary, U.S. Archives.

23. The recommendations were given in the Nicholson report on grazing fees (see Foss 1960:185).

BIBLIOGRAPHY

Box, Thadis W. 1978. "The Arid Lands Revisited—One Hundred Years Since John Wesley Powell." Fifty-Seventh Annual Honor Lecture, Utah State University, Logan, Utah.

Calef, Wesley. 1960. *Private Grazing and Public Lands: Studies of the Local Management of the Taylor Grazing Act.* Chicago: University of Chicago Press.

Clawson, Marion. 1950. *The Western Range Livestock Industry.* New York: McGraw-Hill.

————. 1971. *The Bureau of Land Management.* New York: Praeger Publications.

Foss, Philip. 1960. *Politics and Grass.* Seattle: University of Washington Press.

Gardner, B. Delworth. 1962. "Transfer Restrictions and Misallocation in Grazing Public Range." *American Journal of Agricultural Economics* 44, no. 1 (February):50–63.

Gates, Paul W. 1968. *History of Public Land Law Development.* Washington, D.C.: Public Land Law Review Commission.

Goodsell, Wylie; James R. Gray; and Macie Belfield. 1974. "Southwest Cattle Ranch Organization: Costs and Returns, 1964-1972." *Agricultural Economic Report 255,* USDA Research Service, April.

Ickes, Harold L. 1953-1955. *The Secret Diary of Harold L. Ickes.* 3 vols. New York: Simon and Schuster.

Martin, William E., and William K. Goss. 1963. "Cost-Size Relationships for Southwestern Arizona Cattle Ranches." *Agricultural Experiment Station Bulletin No. 155.* Tucson.

_____. 1978. "Economies of Size and the 160 Acre Limitation: Fact and Fancy." *American Journal of Agricultural Economics* 60 (December): 923-928.

Parr, V.V.; G.W. Collier; and G.S. Klemmendson. 1928. "Ranch Organization and Methods of Livestock Production in the Southwest." *USDA Technical Bulletin* No. 68, June.

Peffer, E. Louise. 1951. *The Closing of the Public Domain.* Stanford: Stanford University Press.

Peltzman, Sam. 1976. "Toward a More General Theory of Regulation." *Journal of Law and Economics* 19:211-240.

Pinchot, Gifford. 1947. *Breaking New Ground.* New York: Harcourt, Brace and Co.

Stigler, George. 1971. "The Theory of Economic Regulation." *The Bell Journal of Economics and Management Science* 2 (Spring): 3-21.

_____. 1975. *The Citizen and the State.* Chicago: University of Chicago Press.

U.S. Budget. 1930-1980.

U.S. Department of Agriculture. 1905. *Annual Report of the Secretary.*

_____. 1936. *The Western Range.* 74th Cong., 2d sess. *Senate Document* 199.

U.S. Department of the Interior. Annual. *Annual Reports* of the Secretary, 1934-1955.

_____. 1936-1941. Grazing Division. *The Grazing Bulletin,* vols. 1-4.

Voigt, William, Jr. 1976. *Public Grazing Lands.* New Brunswick, N.J.: Rutgers University Press.

6 GRAZING RIGHTS AND THE TAYLOR GRAZING ACT, 1960–1980
Bureaucratic Control Over the Range

The Bureau's first responsibility is to secure effective management of all public land values, including rangeland resources. . . . There is, however, very real potential conflict in these management decisions between the short-run interests of the community, the operator himself, and the Nation as a whole in improving the condition of the rangeland resource.

U.S. Department of the Interior (1979a:15)

Grazing permits could only be transferred to BLM-approved buyers —those with commensurate land—and Gardner (1962) has argued that those restrictions prevented allocation of federal land to its highest valued use. In other respects, however, the grazing privileges held by ranchers from 1939 to 1960 were reasonably broad and secure: they were renewed automatically, stocking levels and seasons of use were largely at the discretion of permittees, and user fees were minimal. This legal security allowed ranchers to make managerial decisions to increase the economic returns from the range. That same freedom sharply constrained the role of the Bureau of Land Management. With permittees effectively holding most decision-making authority, bureau employees performed custodial functions—processing permit renewals and transfers and constructing limited land improvements such as roads, fences, wells, and brush removal. The low profile of the BLM in the 1950s is discussed in

case studies by Calef (1960) and Foss (1960) and the general agency
history by Clawson (1971). Those circumstances were hardly prom-
ising for bureaucratic managers concerned with promotion to positions of greater authority, salary, and political power. Programs
which would alter land use patterns were blocked by the political
power of stock owners and a lack of budget appropriations. Accordingly, Interior Department officials had incentive to seek
broader authority over the range and to attenuate the privileges
held by ranchers. The implications for production and wealth of
a shift to bureaucratic control are outlined in the following section.

MAXIMUM ECONOMIC YIELD AND SCIENTIFIC BUREAUCRATIC MANAGEMENT

Ranchers and Interior Department officials have differing incentives
for land use. Stock owners depend directly upon the economic
returns from rangeland for income and wealth. With secure property
rights they can adjust grazing practices in response to market prices,
costs, interest rates, and range conditions to maximize the discounted present value of the land. Among the costs they consider
are the effects on future forage from current harvest (grazing)
practices. To maximize the value of the land and their wealth,
ranchers must continually balance the gains from heavy stocking
one year with the costs from reduced available vegetation the next.
By contrast, Interior Department officials have different concerns.
They cannot increase their wealth through optimal harvest strategies
because they do not receive the resulting returns. Their incomes
depend upon professional job positions and opportunities for advancement which are enhanced by expanding budget appropriations
and staffing levels. Favorable congressional response to budget
requests requires broad agency involvement in land use decisions
to justify expenditure increases. Bureaucratic discretion, though,
conflicts with assignment of secure grazing rights to livestock owners.
Accordingly, the harvest criteria selected by bureaucrats is unlikely
to coincide with that selected by ranchers to maximize the returns
from production. Because they do not bear the costs of reduced
production, Interior officials can select land use practices which
are politically rewarding. These inherent differences in the stocking
practices of ranchers and bureaucrats are illustrated by the hypothetical growth curve in figure 6-1.[1]

Figure 6-1. Forage Growth and Harvest Rates

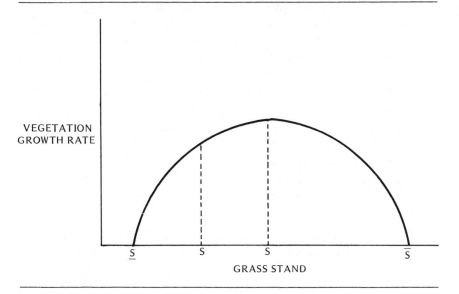

In figure 6-1, forage growth rates, shown by the curve running from S to S̄, depend on the amount of grass existing at any time. The larger the grass stand in the size region S to S*, the greater the growth rate for new vegetation. Beyond S*, increasing the existing stock reduces the growth rate, as crowding occurs and grass competes for soil nutrients, water, and sunshine. At S̄ the growth rate is zero, and a natural equilibrium emerges with a stable grass population in the absence of harvesting and climate changes. At the other end of the scale, if the stock of vegetation is depleted below S, it becomes too limited to replenish itself and dies out. Because of natural growth, grass can be harvested through livestock grazing while maintaining a particular forage stock. The growth curve reveals the maximum which can be harvested from each grass stand without depleting it. For instance, the greatest harvest rate is possible when the grass population equals S*. For larger or smaller levels of vegetation, forage growth is slower and hence harvest rates must fall to maintain the population. S*, then, is the amount of vegetation which allows for maximum sustained yield.

A ranch owner has no necessary reason for harvesting at the maximum sustained yield rate; whether he does depends on whether it is consistent with wealth maximization. Moreover, he may not follow a sustained yield policy. If the pasture has never been grazed and is at the natural equilibrium $\overline{S}$, the ranch owner may heavily stock it with animals and reduce the grass stand to a sustainable level where annual harvests lead to higher returns. Reducing the forage stock from $\overline{S}$ to S^*, for example, allows for more intensive grazing since growth rates are greater. Exogenous forces, though, cause movement to new sustainable levels of forage. A rise in expected livestock prices or interest rates leads ranchers to increase the number of animals placed on the range, further depleting the forage stock. A fall in expected prices brings herd liquidation, light harvesting, and a recovery of vegetation.

This phenomena of adjustable grazing practices in response to market conditions was clearly described in a 1922 study of rangeland use.

> Privately owned grazing lands are not always handled exactly like they would be under government control, because the private individual is seeking the greatest net return from his investment. Thus while a ranchman may decide that the normal carrying capacity of the range is a certain number of animals, he does not limit himself rigidly to the grazing of that number. A policy which produces the greatest amount of forage may not always produce the greatest amount of economic value. For example, a rancher may relatively overstock his ranges under conditions of abnormally high prices with the idea of understocking to rebuild them when prices are low. (Youngblood and Cox 1922:130)

Biological rather than economic criteria for harvesting assist Interior Department officials in achieving larger budgets. Calculating and monitoring biological conditions require a technically trained staff and funding for range surveys, which must be updated from time to time to insure harvest rates are in compliance with biological goals. Closely associated is a necessary regulatory role for the BLM. Ranchers, attempting to increase economic returns, have incentive to avoid, where possible, the constraints imposed by the bureau. If, for example, market and range conditions call for stocking levels beyond the biological limits set by the agency, evasion of the rules is probable; that justifies the hiring of enforcement officials. Enforcement is more likely with a technically trained staff which sees itself as independent of the livestock industry and is organized to accomplish specific range management goals. The importance of a closely knit technical staff was early recognized by Gifford Pinchot (1947) in creating the Forest Service within the Agriculture

Department.[2] The service successfully built a reputation for being scientifically oriented, free of excessive industry influence, and motivated in the public interest. Its popularity helped the Forest Service achieve major budget increases and made it a model to be emulated by the Bureau of Land Management. Finally, arbitrary biological criteria can be manipulated by bureau officials to meet political pressures, since they are not tied to market conditions. That flexibility allows the BLM to cultivate supportive client groups and favorable congressional reviewers. That support is particularly necessary to insulate the agency from the protests of ranchers adversely affected by its regulatory activities.

While it is apparent that ranch owners and bureaucrats would adopt different harvesting policies, in fact the BLM did not have that discretion until after 1960. To use the land in its self-interest, the bureau had to weaken the control of the livestock industry over federal land.

ALLEGATIONS OF OVERGRAZING AND THE CASE FOR GREATER BUREAUCRATIC AUTHORITY

Beginning in 1959 the BLM released data critical of ranchers' past land use practices, which had been allowed because of the bureau's limited regulatory activity. In his 1959 *Annual Report*, Bureau Director Woozley argued that during the period 1954-1958, 19 percent of the range deteriorated, 56 percent was static, and 25 percent improved (U.S. Department of the Interior, *Annual Report of the Director* 1959:303). No bases were given for the figures, and they describe a period of intense drought, blamed in the 1957 and 1958 *Annual Reports* for poor range conditions. Yet in 1959 and thereafter, the reference to drought was dropped and replaced by emphasis on overgrazing by permit holders. The 1960-1963 *Annual Reports* of the secretary of the interior called for greater bureau management to reverse past trends and rehabilitate the range. While similar allegations were repeated through the 1960s, they were highlighted by a 1975 BLM study of Nevada which criticized the wide discretion given permittees over land use, their failure to graze properly, and the neglect of potential uses of rangeland other than ranching (U.S. Department of the Interior 1975). The

Nevada results and other BLM-supplied data were again presented in a 1977 General Accounting Office study sharply critical of relatively unrestricted land use by ranchers:

> The Nation's public rangelands have been deteriorating for years. These vast lands need to be protected through better management by the Bureau of Land Management. Deterioration can be attributed principally to poorly managed grazing by livestock—horses, cattle, sheep, and goats. Livestock have been permitted to graze on public rangelands year after year without adequate regard to the detrimental effect on the range vegetation. . . . (USGAO 1977:i)

The GAO urged intense management to "discontinue destructive continuous grazing" and increased funding and staffing for range rehabilitation (ibid.:iii).

It may seem puzzling that the Bureau of Land Management would release information critical of its own past policies and those of its powerful constituency—information which would make the bureau the center of controversy and subject to intense congressional review.[3] It is generally argued that administrative agencies attempt to keep a low profile and to control information released to Congress during the budgeting process (Lindsay 1975); close scrutiny by Congress upsets that attempt, increasing the possibility that damaging information will be revealed to the public, and thus threatening future appropriations. Given the wide dissemination of the range quality statistics in the *Annual Reports* and the Nevada study, it is clear that the BLM wanted the data made public. Indeed, the land quality reports can be interpreted as an advertising effort by the agency to discredit the existing arrangement that gave overriding authority to ranchers and constrained the regulatory role of the bureau. As early as 1950 BLM's director complained of a lack of personnel to carry out the bureau's mission (see U.S. Department of the Interior, *Annual Reports* of the Director 1950, 1956). Unstated at that time was bureau frustration over the power of the advisory boards relative to BLM officials. The advertised image presented after 1959 was one of the public's rangeland deteriorating under intense grazing pressure by uncaring or, at minimum, unknowing permittees seeking to maximize their private income at the public expense. Reversal of alleged trends would require greater regulation of private use of federal land and significant investment in range improvements—reseeding, brush removal, fencing, and well construction. The case was being made for scientific bureaucratic management and associated increases in budget allocations and staffing for the BLM. Certainly the 1977 GAO report brought congressional attention to BLM complaints that inadequate funding and employment were paralyzing the bureau and preventing it from meeting its congressional mandate to preserve the federal range.

The BLM statistics pointing to deteriorating land quality are controversial, and there is little data to judge their accuracy. The bases of the statistics—timing, the role of precipitation levels, and definitions of deteriorating, static, and improving—are not presented in the reports. Range survey results are sensitive to when they are taken. Those made at the end of a grazing season when rainfall has been sparse will naturally show poor conditions; they, however, do not represent trends, and time trends of conditions reported by Box (1978) do not show deterioration. Moreover, precipitation appears to be a crucial factor in determining the density and vigor of forage. The 1950s were a period of chronic drought in much of the West. When rainfall improved, forage growth rates rebounded. Dependence of range production upon rainfall is discussed by Cook and Sims (1975), and Le Houerou and Hoste (1977).

Repeated in the bureau's discussion of range conditions are references to a pristine, natural condition of thick healthy grass stands prior to the advent of livestock grazing in the West (see, for example, references to past conditions in U.S. Department of the Interior 1979b:iii, 1; 1979c:2-2). That would correspond to $\overline{S}$ in figure 6-1. Though the BLM does not explicitly argue for a return to a natural equilibrium with no grazing, there is a definite emphasis on "rehabilitation" toward some hypothetical biological goal. Yet it is unclear that the western range was ever the land of tall grass envisioned in the bureau's hypothetical alternative to current conditions. A recent review of nineteenth century journals and diaries of early pioneers by Vale (1975) reveals that much of the arid Intermountain West was dominated by shrubs. Limited grass stands were confined near streams. Vast sagebrush areas, commonly cited as evidence of overgrazing, appear to have existed well before the introduction of livestock to the range. Vale argues that attempts to eradicate brush and reseed cannot be justified in terms of reestablishing a natural equilibrium. The land deterioration conditions cited by the BLM, then, likely reflect long-standing trends of natural erosion which could be altered only at high social cost. Stevens and Godfrey (1972:618, 619) calculated rates of return for plowing, reseeding, brush eradication, and fence construction for the 6.5-million-acre Vale District in eastern Oregon. They found that the expenditures could not be justified ex post since rates of return were well below the opportunity costs of capital.

Given the record of secure tenure held by ranchers from 1934 through 1960, it is unlikely they would have harvested to reduce the present value of the range resource. As argued earlier, biological and economic criteria for grazing are not the same; hence, regulators concerned with maximizing environmental quality will call for stocking levels which differ from those preferred by ranchers. There is, though, other evidence indicating that stock owners have not been myopic in their harvest practices. BLM lands are rarely stocked to their authorized capacity. Annually, permittees apply for voluntary nonuse status for portions of their total stocking authorizations when range and market conditions are poor. Nonuse status is crucial because, ironically, failure to fully stock the range carries the threat of a formal and permanent cut in stocking authorization by the BLM. The BLM also imposes involuntary nonuse on permittees as part of range management programs. Unfortunately, available data do not separate voluntary and involuntary cuts, though discussions with BLM personnel indicate that voluntary cuts are common. Table 6-1 lists nonuse as a percent of actual stocking on BLM lands for selected western states. The resulting percentages are high, suggesting that restraint is used in herding practices.

Finally, range conditions are affected by investment, and the struggle between ranchers and bureau officials for tenure control of the range appears to have reduced investment on BLM lands. In arid regions it is vital to spread cattle to avoid bunching, a practice which leads to local overgrazing and trampling of grass stands, while remote areas remain untouched. Spreading requires expenditures on wells and fencing, and BLM lands seem to have had less investment than comparable private land, but research on the issue has been limited (see Godfrey [1972] and Stevens and Godfrey [1972]). Bureau expenditures have been traditionally tied to grazing fees, which have provided limited revenue. Ranchers have opposed grazing fee increases and preferred private investment. Fee revenues to finance investment are not earmarked to a particular area; hence,

Table 6–1. Nonuse as a Percent of Actual Stocking

State	1962	1963	1964	1965	1966	1967	1968	1969	1970	1971	1972	1973	1974	1975	1976
Arizona	12	17	18	9	10	19	25	23	22	19	18	23	28	24	9
Colorado	25	9	15	12	10	10	10	11	15	16	19	19	21	25	22
Nevada	44	42	39	40	42	40	34	31	33	32	33	31	19	34	20
New Mexico	16	12	14	17	18	13	10	11	13	19	23	19	17	17	17
Utah	36	38	38	33	29	26	24	26	26	33	35	38	33	31	28
Wyoming	22	22	20	18	17	16	17	16	26	32	26	30	27	27	22

Source: Calculated from U.S. Department of the Interior, Bureau of Land Management, *Public Lands Statistics.*

a rancher is unlikely to benefit from his contribution. Moreover, federal investment increases the government's claim on the land. Private investment, on the other hand, tends to tie an area to the permittee, an effect recognized early by the solicitor (see chapter 5) and by the comptroller general in the 1977 GAO report (pp. 10-11). Accordingly, the BLM has not encouraged private investment, which has fallen sharply as BLM managerial control over the range has expanded. BLM *Public Lands Statistics* for 1961-1976 reveal this decline: during the 1960s private investment accounted for an average of 44 percent of the wells dug annually and 30 percent of fences built; from 1971 to 1976 private investment accounted for an annual average of only 11 percent of new wells and 8 percent of new fences.

GRAZING FEES AND THE CASE FOR GREATER BUREAUCRATIC AUTHORITY

Low user fees provided additional pressure to attenuate the privileges held by permit holders over federal land. Low grazing fees paid by permittees on BLM land relative to those charged by the Forest Service reinforced the image projected by the bureau that ranchers were selfishly using the range in disregard for the public interest: not only were they plundering federal lands by overgrazing, but they were being subsidized to do so.

User fees had been held down since 1934 by the political power of the western livestock industry. Defeat of the Interior Department's efforts to raise levies in 1946 and the subsequent reorganization of the Grazing Service into the BLM left a legacy that continued through 1960. Limited increases were agreed to in 1950 and 1955 by the National Advisory Board Council (the national rancher advisory board) to mitigate criticism that fees were too low. The General Accounting Office in 1954 and 1961 called for fee hikes and a shift to market forage values in calculating the fee. Similar statements were made by the Bureau of the Budget in 1957, 1959, and 1964 (USDA and U.S. Department of the Interior 1977: 2-11, 2-13). Pressure continued to mount for further adjustments as congressional attention focused on rangeland following the release of BLM data on land quality. During congressional review of user charges in 1969, BLM Director Rasmussen argued that low fees helped to create a sense of proprietary rights among permittees (U.S. Department of the Interior, *Annual Report* of the Director 1969:118). Significantly, organized criticism of the fee structure was made by conservation groups such as the National Wildlife Federation and the Izaak Walton League (see U.S. House 1969). Conservationists were emerging as potent lobby supporters in the bureau's efforts to weaken rancher authority over the range. Congress called for fees equal to market values in the Federal Land Policy and Management Act of 1976. Indeed, the act called for a thorough review of levies charged by the Interior and Agriculture Departments. The fee issue continued to be raised in 1976 and 1977 Interior Department appropriation hearings (USDA and U.S. Department of the Interior 1977:2-24). As figure 6-2 shows, the effect of that attention was to raise BLM fees to levels comparable to those charged by the Forest Service.

Higher user fees were in the Interior Department's interest. Greater fees brought increased revenue for discretionary expenditure on land investment, expenditures which could be tailored to reward influential groups; higher fees weakened the alleged proprietary rights held by ranchers, and their resistance made more credible the view that private interests were thwarting those of the public; finally, increased fees mitigated criticism in the department's budgeting process, smoothing efforts to raise appropriations.

Despite unfavorable publicity ranchers had an incentive to fight the proposed fee hikes because they brought wealth losses. The difference between the value of the range and the present value of fee charges was capitalized into ranch sales prices, since sales included BLM permits. Those purchasing ranches, then, paid for the full expected value of the forage. Any unexpected fee increases not considered in negotiating the sale would bring a wealth loss to the buyer equal to the capitalized increase. In resisting fee increases, ranchers placed political pressure on the Interior Department through the Senate and House Committees on Interior and Insular Affairs. They successfully achieved delays in the implementation of new hikes, but they could not prevent them. It is likely that Interior supported the delays as a means of defusing political opposition. Changes in the formula for calculating user charges to bring them to full market value were to be phased in over ten years beginning in 1969. Four moritoriums on fee increases, however, were adopted in 1970, 1972, 1975, and 1977 (USDA and

Figure 6-2. Grazing Fees per Cow per Month (current dollars)

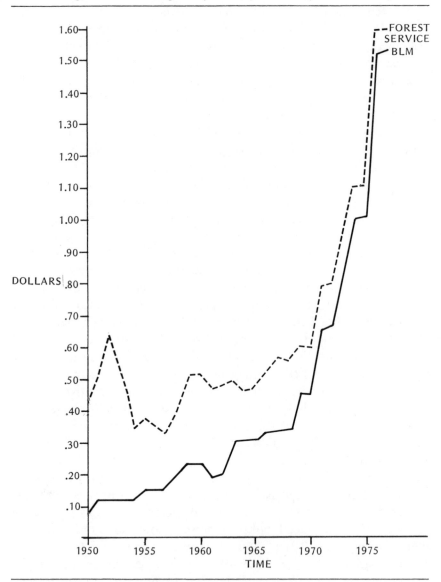

Source: USDA and U.S. Department of the Interior (1977).

U.S. Department of the Interior 1977:2-29). Nevertheless, the fee increases were visible evidence of erosion of the tenure arrangements stock owners held over federal rangeland.

MAJOR LEGISLATIVE CHANGES ATTENUATING GRAZING PRIVILEGES

Sympathetic Lobby Support—The Interior Department and Conservation Groups

BLM efforts to weaken rancher control over public land, through allegations of misuse, underpayment, and single interest domination, were assisted by conservation groups. Prior to the Taylor Grazing Act, conservationists opposed the transfer of federal land to the western states or private parties. (Voigt [1976:99–131] brings out the conservationist view of public land policy.) After the act was passed, they unsuccessfully fought the delegation of authority to the advisory boards; conservation groups lobbied against efforts to sell Interior lands in 1947 and 1948 after the collapse of the Grazing Service.[4] Relatively ineffective in the 1950s, conservation groups were bolstered in the 1960s by a rise in popular concern for environmental quality, recreation, and conservation of natural resources. High real incomes not only increased demand for environmental quality, but made the population more mobile, spurting the demand for recreation on federal lands. Popular pressure grew for the establishment of additional national parks, campgrounds, wilderness, and wildlife areas (see Clawson 1971:109–120). This environment revitalized old conservation groups and led to the formation of new ones, such as the Izaak Walton League, the Sierra Club, and the Natural Resources Defense Council. Conservation groups, then, competed with ranchers for federal land. Socially costly lobbying was a direct outcome of the failure to assign property rights to rangeland in 1934. Since fee title was absent, voluntary market trading could not occur and access to land depended on bureaucratic allocation and political lobbying. Conservationists joined the Interior Department in seeking constraints on livestock operations and multiple use guarantees.[5] With the secretary of the interior and the director of the BLM, they testified in favor of legislation increasing the bureau's regulatory activities. The BLM could only be an effective broker among competing claimants if the constraints placed on the agency were removed. Conservationist interest in BLM lands stems more from general philosophical views than from inherent qualities of the land. BLM lands are typically arid brush and grassland suitable for grazing, but with few of the park-like qualities commonly associated with some national forest areas. Philosophical goals of conservationists are outlined in general by Barnett and Morse (1963:72–100) and in particular for rangeland by Voigt (1976:99–131).

The political power of conservation groups was rising during the 1960s, while that of ranchers was declining, likely due to demographic patterns. From 1930 through 1950 stock owners were influential with the Public Lands Committees of the House and Senate where western representatives were dominant. Their constituents were rural. In 1940 for instance, seven of the eleven far western states had populations which were over 50 percent rural. By 1970 that pattern had changed, with all eleven states having populations over 50 percent urban (U.S. Department of Commerce 1930-1970). More urban voters, concerned with recreation possibilities and with limited ties to the livestock industry, no doubt diluted industry influence with western representatives.

Legislation Affecting Grazing Privileges

Beginning in 1964 major legislative changes were made in the management and allocation of federal rangeland. The impact was cumulative, so that by 1980 ranchers no longer held secure proprietary rights to the federal range. The thrust of the legislation was to increase discretionary authority for the interior secretary and the BLM director in assigning and regulating use privileges. The result was a dramatic expansion in the functions and budgets of the BLM. The bureau was more than a coincidental beneficiary of the legislation, and the legislation was not merely the result of conservationist pressure. The land quality data released by the agency provided support for the conservationist-BLM plea for greater regulation, and the data were referenced in wording proposed legislation. The interior secretary and the BLM director testified for favored bills; and in some cases the agency drafted them.

Classification and Multiple Use Act of 1964 (PL 88-607)

This act provided the framework for bureaucratic reallocation of rangeland. The Taylor Grazing Act emphasized the livestock industry and the use of federal land for grazing purposes. Increasing the value of production was encouraged.[6] Under the Taylor Act stock owners ultimately obtained near property rights to the range. The Multiple Use Act of 1964 marked a reversal of those conditions. The act called for reallocation of federal land from single use (livestock) to multiple use. Moreover, the emphasis on maximizing the production value of the range was dropped; in assigning access privileges consideration was to be "given to the relative values of the various resources and not necessarily to the combination of uses that will give the greatest dollar return or the greatest unit output." Land management was to be based on biological, sustained yield principles, not economic criteria to achieve multiple use goals.

While the law was a general statement of principles without specific policy directives, it influenced the tenor of subsequent legislation as well as the actions of administrative agencies. During congressional consideration the bill was actively supported by Interior Secretary Udall and BLM Director Stoddard. Udall stressed the need to formally recognize the demands of non-livestock groups for range use (see U.S. Senate [1964a] for testimony of Udall, Stoddard, and others). Livestock associations understandably voiced concern over the implications of the bill, but could not prevent its passage.

Public Land Law Review Commission Act of 1964 (PL 88-606) and the National Environmental Policy Act of 1969 (PL 91-190)

These two statutes continued the general policy changes of the 1960s, and they reflect the widespread interest in conservation issues during that time. For instance, in the Ninetieth Congress over one hundred bills were introduced regarding the environment (U.S. Senate 1969, 1971). The Public Land Law Review Commission Act showed the concern of Congress over the condition of federal lands in light of the data presented by the BLM and the increased demand for access. *Senate Report 1444* on the legislation stated that a chief deficiency of the Taylor Grazing Act was its failure to give the secretary of the interior guidelines (and authority) for balancing "competing demands for the same piece of land" (U.S. Senate 1964b). The National Environmental Policy

Act mandated that all federal agencies consider environmental quality in policy decisions. That provided statutory authority for the secretary to review current arrangements and proposed management plans to reverse the asserted land deterioration.

Federal Land Policy and Management Act of 1976 (PL 94-579)

All told this act, more than any other, fundamentally changed the nature of federal policy regarding rangeland. It dropped the Taylor Grazing Act's implication that federal ownership was to be temporary, and instead called for long-run management of the range for sustained yield and multiple use. As part of that mandate, the functions of the BLM as a permanent regulatory agency were outlined for the first time. To implement them section 201 of the law required a systematic range survey and inventory to increase the information available for more intense bureaucratic management. Section 401 directly referenced the land deterioration figures released earlier by the BLM as evidence of the need for major rehabilitation programs. In addition, grazing fees were to be reviewed to insure that forage values were properly included. Section 402 authorized the secretary of the interior to modify or suspend grazing permits as punishment for rule violation, increasing his enforcement powers while reducing the discretion available to ranchers. The secretary was also allowed to offer short-term licenses rather than ten-year permits when they were in the "interest of sound land management." Short-term licenses gave the secretary greater control over annual stocking levels; they also reduced the security of tenure held by ranchers.

The licenses or annual permits were used to implement allotment management plans. Allotments were the pasture areas assigned individual permittees, though occasionally more than one permittee used the same area. Beginning in the late 1960s, stocking controls and land rehabilitation plans were drawn for individual allotments. They, however, were voluntary and implemented only on a limited basis until the enactment of the Federal Land Policy and Management Act. Section 402 made the allotment management plans mandatory, with formal statutory directives and timetables for completion. The plans required that the secretary specify the number of animals to be grazed and season of use, and that he modify harvest practices as necessary to restore the range and meet multiple use criteria.

Those directives usurped powers previously assumed by the influential grazing advisory boards. Further, the boards lost their legal mandate; they were made optional by the act, repealing the Taylor Act amendments of 1939 and 1949, which had made local, state, and national advisory boards mandatory. By contrast, multiple use advisory boards were created with representatives of various potential users besides livestock owners. The optional grazing boards could be established by petition of a majority of a district's permit holders, but they were to last no longer than to 1985. The weakened boards were terminated by the secretary in 1978, though they were temporarily reinstated for five years with limited advisory roles later that year.[7] The dismantling of the once-powerful advisory boards was testimony to the relative decline of rancher authority over the land they grazed in the 1970s. Secretary Ickes had unsuccessfully attempted to constrain them in the 1930s and 1940s, and their influence over land policy likely explains the ambivalent support of ranchers for proposed public land sales in 1947 and 1948. Yet political conditions changed, and the ability of ranchers to protect the boards dropped, pointing to the inherent tenuousness of property rights held subject to bureaucratic control and allocation.

The Interior Department did more than lobby for the Federal Land Policy and Management Act which so broadly increased the department's authority. The secretary's testimony before the House and Senate Committees on Interior and Insular Affairs indicates that the department drafted the legislation. That action is consistent with the view that bureaucracies are not mere passive respondents to congressional policies, but attempt to mold those policies in their self-interest.[8] Conservation groups joined Interior Secretary Kleppe and BLM Director Berklund in lobbying for the bill, citing bureau reports on land deterioration. Representatives of the Sierra Club, the Wilderness Society, and the Wildlife Federation called for more restrictive grazing permits, arguing that long-term, automatically renewed contracts gave stock owners vested rights which limited other users' access to public lands. The potency of the conservation lobby is reflected by its appearance at legislative hearings. The House Committee on Interior and Insular Affairs conducted hearings in the eleven far western states in 1974 on an early draft of the Federal Land Policy and Management Act. During those hearings testimony was given by or received from 335 witnesses. Of those, 215 or nearly 65 percent represented conservation or recreation groups.[9]

As might be expected, livestock interests unsuccessfully protested the unilateral imposition of allotment management plans on permit holders, the proposed increase in grazing fees, and the planned termination of the grazing advisory boards.

Public Rangeland Improvement Act of 1978 (PL 95-514)

This law supplemented the Federal Land Policy and Management Act by reemphasizing the deterioration in public land quality and the need for scientific management. The act authorized $365 million over twenty years for range rehabilitation by the BLM through the allotment management plans. During that time the secretary was authorized to reduce stocking levels and shorten the term of permits while carrying out the management plans. The plans were to comply with environmental impact statements (EIS) required by the National Environmental Policy Act. The EIS process provided for public hearings and third party (non-permit holders) input into the development of the allotment management plans. The hearings were a forum by which conservation groups could build public pressure on the bureau to respond to their demands. While conservationists were important allies for the BLM in constraining grazing privileges, their interests did not always coincide with those of the bureau, a point to be further examined.

Allotment Management Plans

As they are implemented, allotment management plans greatly limit the use privileges held by ranchers. Drawn by the bureau, they impose long-term stocking cuts of as much as 30 percent on permit holders and place restrictions on land use as pastures are withdrawn from grazing for rehabilitation.[10] As forage growth responds, more is allocated to wildlife under multiple use concepts.

The required stock reductions are for up to twenty years to allow plant stocks to expand. However, the forage response to reduced grazing is problematic, since it is vitally affected by highly variable precipitation in the West. Therefore, permit holders are uncertain as to the actual length of the imposed cuts. Moreover, the emphasis of bureaucratic managers on achieving targeted biological sustained-yield goals conflict with more flexible harvest practices desired by ranchers. The allotment plans, then, impose wealth losses on permittees. To the extent that the market signals followed by ranchers reflect social preferences and costs, bureaucratic interference reduces production and wealth.

Tension Between the BLM and Conservation Groups in Implementing Legislation

Because the Bureau of Land Management and its conservation supporters faced different political costs, and because conservationists sought to control the agency in their interests as ranchers had done, conflict between the two emerged after 1973.

In compliance with the National Environmental Policy Act directive that "unquantified amenities and values be given appropriate consideration in decision-making along with economic and technical considerations," the BLM prepared a single environmental impact statement for its allotment management plans. The nature of the management plans were of vital concern to conservation groups demanding greater emphasis on recreation and wildlife. In 1973 the Natural Resources Defense Council (NRDC) filed suit in federal court arguing that a single plan was insufficient, that site-specific impact statements for each covered area in the plans were necessary, and that the bureau should more rapidly implement them (*NRDC v. Morton,* 388 Fed. Supp. 829). The court concurred and ordered 212 (later reduced to 144) environmental impact statements. The order specifically required that alternatives to livestock grazing be included and that the environmental effects of grazing be documented. Once again the court referenced the BLM data on land deterioration as evidence of the need for site-specific statements. In 1978 the Natural Resources Defense Council returned to court (*NRDC v. Andrus,* memorandum opinion of the U.S. District Court, Civil Action No. 1983-73), charging the BLM was not preparing impact statements and developing management programs rapidly enough. The court responded by ordering a timetable from the agency for completion.

Through court action the Natural Resources Defense Council appears to have forced stricter and more rapid adoption of limits on livestock grazing than the BLM would otherwise have desired. Immediate, extensive land use controls are sure to trigger political reaction from ranching groups. Accordingly, the agency would prefer to mitigate those effects by delaying the moderating stock reductions as long as bureau authority is firmly established. BLM officials would also desire flexibility in responding to the demands of competing user groups to insure political support and would therefore want to avoid entanglements placed by any client group. The conflict between the BLM and conservationists reflects the tradeoff in costs and benefits faced by administrative agencies in responding to new political conditions. They must react to the demands of new, supportive client groups while minimizing the political costs from those adversely affected (see Peltzman 1976).

BUREAUCRATIC RESTRICTIONS ON GRAZING PRIVILEGES: THE CASE OF THE RIO PUERCO, EAST SOCORRO, AND EAST ROSWELL BLM AREAS IN NEW MEXICO

The regulatory environment brought by the legislation and the allotment management plans since 1960 is unprecedented for the Bureau of Land Management, and it reflects the control bureau managers now have relative to ranchers. The impact is illustrated by the experience in the Rio Puerco, East Socorro, and East Roswell areas of New Mexico. The three include 22 percent of all BLM land in the state, and 9 percent of the state's total land. They are among the first areas in the U.S. scheduled for complete adoption of allotment management plans.

There are currently 387 permit holders on 403 allotments in the three areas, and most will be part of the imposed plans.[11] In 1975 permit holders in the Rio Puerco area were notified of impending controls on pasture use, stocking cuts, and consolidation of some allotments. Meetings were held on the details in the spring of 1976, and public hearings were conducted the following year.

Allotment plans were to begin in 1979. These efforts to achieve voluntary compliance of permittees with the plans were designed to reduce resistance and political opposition and to allow ranchers to seek alternative sources of land. Similar procedures were followed in the East Socorro and East Roswell areas.

Under the mandatory allotment plans, the bureau proposes immediate stock reductions of approximately 11 percent in the Rio Puerco, 28 percent in the East Roswell, and 30 percent in the East Socorro.[12] Stocking will be gradually resumed as vegetation increases. The BLM predicts plant stock increases of 37 percent in twenty years in East Socorro. Total livestock production will eventually be allowed to grow 2 percent beyond current levels, with the remainder of the land left for wildlife and a larger equilibrium plant stock (U.S. Department of the Interior 1979c:i). By the year 2000 forage available for livestock in the Rio Puerco and East Roswell areas is anticipated to rise by 58 percent and 57 percent respectively.[13] Those targets, which are uncertain at best, are to be achieved through grazing schedules which limit or remove pastures from livestock use. For instance, each of 1.5 million acres in the East Roswell area will be rested one year out of every four, retiring large amounts of land from livestock production. This factor is particularly significant for ranchers who are dependent on federal land for forage. In the East Roswell area, an average of 61 percent of ranch land is federally owned. The length of the stocking cuts depends on the response of the plant stock to grazing limits and precipitation levels.[14] Many permittees feel they will be permanent, as reflected in testimony in *Valdez v. Applegate* (U.S. District Court for New Mexico, CV. 78-9440). Those reductions impose significant income losses for ranchers; for instance, the BLM estimates that gross ranch income will fall 50 percent in East Roswell during the 1980s. Those losses are privately born by ranchers, not bureau personnel. Ironically, BLM data for the area show 1979 calving rates in excess of 80 percent and calf-selling weights averaging 430-460 pounds, statistics generally associated with productive, not deteriorated, land (U.S. Department of the Interior 1979b:3-60). The drastic stocking cuts imposed by the BLM, despite assertions by ranchers that the land is not overgrazed, underscore the divergent management philosophies of maximizing economic yield and of maintaining biological criteria.

Individual permittee control over land use is also reduced by the consolidation of small allotments into large community allotments of several permittees. Consolidation is most significant in the Rio Puerco where average permit size is smallest. In 1979 there were 96 allotments which are to be reduced to 61, forcing individuals to share the same pasture areas (U.S. Department of the Interior 1978:A–14). There are serious costs from community arrangements: mixing the registered and unregistered livestock of various permittees raises the costs of selective breeding to improve herds; group use of pastures reduces the incentive for particular permittees to limit grazing pressure to build up forage. Such practices must be jointly agreed to and enforced. Group decision making is also necessary for sharing maintenance expenses for fences, gates, and other investments. Since such decisions are costly to reach and enforce, less private investment and maintenance is the probable result of consolidation. Existing community allotments in Rio Puerco have a record of coordination problems and poor fencing.[15]

IMPACT OF ATTENUATED GRAZING PRIVILEGES ON RANCH VALUES

The substitution of biological for economic criteria in land management reduces the net present value of the land if constraints are placed on the ability of ranchers to respond to market signals. Further, values also decline if there is uncertainty as to future regulatory policies. Those effects are reflected in the sale price of ranches where BLM land is included. The proportion of BLM land to total ranch acreage varies, but in some cases is nearly 100 percent, though figures near 60 percent are more common (U.S. Department of the Interior 1979b: table A–2). One would anticipate that under current conditions ranch values would rise with the proportion of deeded acreage.

To test that hypothesis, grazing fees, sales, and acreage data for 145 New Mexico ranches sold from 1970 to 1978 were collected and converted to 1967 dollars.[16] Since ranch size and land quality varied, prices were standardized by dividing by the number of cattle which could be raised on each ranch, giving the price paid for the land necessary to raise one cow. Those prices were

Table 6-2. Statistical Test of the Impact of Deeded Acreage on
Ranch Values (t-statistics are in parentheses)

Price = 446.89a + 11.11 Deeded + 158.34 Grazing Fee
        (1.91)   (13.46)   (.49)
R^2 =   .58, F (2.141) = 96.94
DW =   2.03
N^a = 144.00

---

[a]The Cochrane-Orcutt Iterative Technique was used to adjust for autocorrelation and as a result one observation was lost.

regressed against the percentage of deeded acreage, grazing fees, and a constant to see if the proportion of privately owned land affected sales values. The results are shown in table 6-2, and they are consistent with the hypotheses: prospective buyers preferred ranches where property rights were secure, offering less for those subject to BLM regulations. The average sales price per cow for the nine-year period was $1,137, and the statistical test indicates that prices rose by $11 for each increase in the percent of deeded acreage.

Similar results are reported in another study of New Mexico data by Fowler and Gray (1980). They compared appraisal values for BLM and Forest Service permits for the period 1965-1979. They found BLM permit values generally exceeded those of the Forest Service until after 1973, whereupon they fell relative to Forest Service appraisals. Both Forest Service and BLM permit values declined in real terms relative to the price of private land. Those findings support the view that greater bureaucratic regulation by both agencies occurred after 1965, but that BLM policies were less restrictive and uncertain until 1973. That situation changed with new legislation and the prospect of widespread adoption of allotment management plans.

IMPACT OF BUREAUCRATIC CONTROL ON THE BLM BUDGET AND STAFF

Budget Effects

Both the theory presented in chapter 2 and the empirical evidence outlined in chapters 5 and 6 argue that broad rancher authority in land use decisions restricted the growth of the Bureau of Land Management. Therefore, the budget should have expanded as the regulatory role of the BLM grew in the 1970s. The bureau budget from fiscal years 1947 to 1977 is shown in figure 6-3 in constant 1967 dollars. The pattern is instructive. While not as flat as one

Figure 6-3. Bureau of Land Management Budget (1967 dollars)

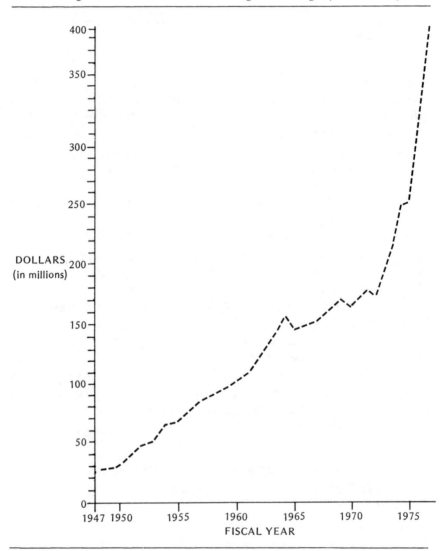

Source: U.S. Budgets.

might have predicted, the bureau budget follows a time trend which does not change until fiscal year 1972. After than BLM appropriations rise dramatically. The record corresponds with the historical relationship between permit holders and the agency. When ranchers successfully limited BLM functions, the budget rose gradually. The increase occurs after bureau advertisements to discredit rancher control and during major legislative changes, broadening the scope of regulation. The Classification and Multiple Use Act of 1964, the National Environmental Policy Act of 1969, and the Report of the Public Land Law Review Commission in 1970 preceed the jump, but the Federal Land Policy and Management Act of 1976 and the Public Rangeland Improvement Act of 1978 follow it. The latter two statutes provide for the most extensive intervention in land use by the BLM.

To more precisely examine the pattern shown in figure 6-3, statistical tests were run to determine the relationship between allocations for the agency and the federal budget. A statistically significant change in the relationship between the two after 1972 would strongly support the contention that the bureau benefited from legislative changes by receiving a greater share of the federal budget. Two regressions were run with the results given in tables 6-3 and 6-4. In the first case, the BLM budget was regressed against time, the federal budget, and a constant, where all values were in 1967 dollars.

The results in table 6-3 show a significant relationship between the growth of the federal budget and bureau appropriations. To see if the pattern changed in the 1970s, a shift term and two additional time and federal budget variables were added after 1972. The shift term was a dummy variable with the value zero prior to 1972 and one thereafter. If significant, it would reveal a change in the intercept of the estimated equation after 1972. The new time

Table 6-3. The Effect of Time and the Federal Budget on the BLM Budget (t-statistics are in parentheses)

BLM Budget = −69.65 + 1.39 Federal Budget + 1.06 Time
                 (−2.51) (2.24)   (.30)

R^2 = .88
DW = .5
N = 31.00

Table 6-4. Changes in the Relationship Between the BLM Budget, the Federal Budget, and Time (t-statistics are in parentheses)

BLM Budget = 24.00 + 8.87 Time + 35.97 New Time
              (1.87) (6.06)   (3.01)
              −   .37 Federal Budget + .25 New Federal Budget
              (−1.38)   (.22)
              − 1014.78 Shift
                 (−8.21)

R^2 = .99
DW = 1.78
N = 31.00

variable had the value zero through 1971 and then took the values 26 through 31 for the remaining six years of the time series. It was included to see if time had an added effect on the BLM budget after 1972, suggesting a different time trend. Similarly, the new federal budget variable was included to test if that budget had an added effect on BLM appropriations after 1971. The value of the new federal variable was zero until 1972 and then equal to annual federal expenditures from 1972 through 1977.

With the addition of the new variables in table 6-4, the explanatory power of the estimated equation increases, but only the time variables and the shift term are significant at the .025 level. The results show it is impossible to clearly separate the effects of time and federal budget on BLM appropriations. The two series are closely related, with the correlation coefficient for time and the federal budget equal to .98. Nevertheless, the second equation indicates a structural change in the relationship between BLM appropriations and time and the federal budget from 1972 through 1977.[17] A Chow test using the sum of squared residuals for the two equations gives $F_{(3,25)} = 7.34$, which is significant at the 1 percent level (Chow 1960:591-605). The Chow test shows that the estimated relationship between the BLM budget and the independent variables significantly changed after 1972.

Table 6-5 provides illustrative data detailing the rise in the share of the federal budget going to the BLM after 1972, as bureaucratic control expanded.

Table 6-5. BLM Appropriations as a Percent of the Federal Budget

Year	Percent	Year	Percent
1947	.036	1963	.105
1948	.046	1964	.122
1949	.047	1965	.105
1950	.051	1966	.093
1951	.045	1967	.087
1952	.049	1968	.092
1953	.056	1969	.098
1954	.073	1970	.093
1955	.075	1971	.093
1956	.080	1972	.091
1957	.087	1973	.104
1958	.084	1974	.123
1959	.093	1975	.116
1960	.094	1976	.143
1961	.092	1977	.173
1962	.108		

Source: U.S. Budgets.

Effects on the Size and Composition of the BLM Staff

To manage range use in keeping with biological criteria, the bureau must have a technically trained staff. Such training lends credibility to BLM management reports and helps the agency control information released to congressional appropriations and oversight committees. Also, such a staff is more likely to identify with the technical-biological goals of the bureau than the profit-maximizing interests of the ranchers. The importance of staff outlook was seen early by both permit holders and Interior officials, but ranchers were able to amend the Taylor Grazing Act, forcing the agency to hire individuals with practical (not technical) experience—a means of securing a staff at least knowledgeable of ranching. It was not a coincidence that Grazing Service Director Carpenter, a rancher, was sympathetic to the industry, while subsequent Directors Rutledge and Forsling, both hired from the Forest Service, were at odds with the range livestock industry. The need for a professional staff was

Figure 6-4. Bureau of Land Management[a] Employment

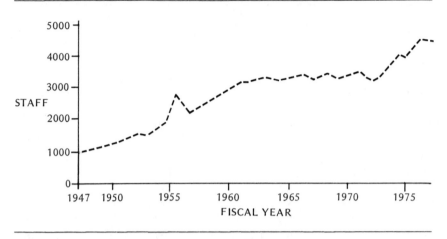

[a]Management of Lands and Resources
Source: U.S. Budgets.

stressed during the 1950s in the *Annual Reports* of the secretary of the interior.

While time series data on the composition of the staff are not available, current evidence shows that the BLM has been successful in obtaining employees with scientific training to implement legislation passed since 1964. For example, range conservationists are responsible for implementing bureau programs at the grazing district level. Of the 469 range conservationists employed in 1979, 80 percent had at least a bachelor's degree in range management. At the BLM Rangeland Management Division, where specific policies are made, all twelve staff members have range management degrees.[18] Of the upper level management positions filled from 1973 to 1976 (state director, associate state director, district manager, assistant district manager), approximately 80 percent of the successful applicants had range or forestry degrees.[19]

The sharp rise in budget appropriations since 1972, during an expansion of the bureau's legislative mandate, was accompanied by an increase in staff size. Figure 6-4 details the number of permanent employees for management of lands and resources from the *U.S. Budget.* From 1947 through 1972 there is a gradual increase in the agency's size, though the number of employees is essentially flat from 1962 to 1972. Beyond that year the number rises, reflecting the greater managerial role of the BLM.

A SHORT SUMMARY

In summarizing events from 1960 through 1980, there is a clear shift in authority and emphasis regarding federal rangeland. Ranchers have lost much of the security of tenure and decision-making power held prior to 1960 under the Taylor Grazing Act. The beneficiaries of the shift have been the Bureau of Land Management and its conservationist supporters. Ranch values have fallen in relative terms where BLM land is a significant share of total acreage, while bureau budgets and staffing have risen. Conservation groups have received greater access through multiple use guarantees. While changes in the regulatory environment were facilitated by general concern for environmental issues, Interior officials were protagonists—circulating reports, testifying, and drafting legislation to expand their regulatory role. Those actions follow the model of bureaucratic behavior used throughout this study of property rights to western land.

NOTES

1. This discussion builds on the model of renewable resource use outlined by Quirk (1976:333-343).
2. See Pinchot's organizational philosophy and call for scientific management in Pinchot (1947).
3. Voigt (1976:318) voices surprise that critical data was "leaked," failing to see that the data was in the BLM's interest.
4. Also see Voigt (1976:203-220) on efforts to sell federal lands in the late 1940s and early 1950s.
5. Peffer (1951:281, 324-330) outlines the conservationist conflict with ranchers.
6. The emphasis in livestock production in management of BLM lands was repeated in the *Annual Reports* of the Secretary of the Interior and Director of the BLM as late as 1950-1954. After that, references to the need to promote the industry are dropped.
7. Laitala (1975) briefly outlines the history of the grazing advisory boards.
8. In a letter from Secretary of the Interior Kleppe to Representative Haley, dated 28 April 1976, Kleppe refers to legislation drafted by the department and submitted to Congress with the recommendation for passage. See U.S. House (1976:53).

    Consistent Interior support for the proposed legislation is reflected in earlier hearings as well. In 1975 Assistant Secretary of the Interior Horton attacked previous arrangements while emphasizing sustained yield and multiple use (U.S. Senate 1975). Director Berklund criticized single use of public lands (U.S. House 1975).

9. U.S. House (1974). Included were traditional environmental groups such as the Sierra Club and the Wilderness Society, wildlife groups, and recreational organizations.

10. See, for example, the allotment management plans discussed for three New Mexico regions (U.S. Department of the Interior 1978, 1979b, 1979c). Some 1,164 allotment management plans were negotiated between the BLM and permittees in the late 1960s. No further action to implement additional plans followed until enactment of the Federal Land Policy and Management Act of 1976. Under that law seven thousand additional plans were to be implemented beginning in 1980 (Mr. David Little, Rangelands Management Division, BLM; also U.S. Department of the Interior 1979a).

11. The Rio Puerco, East Socorro, and East Roswell resource areas are portions of the Albuquerque, Socorro, and Roswell BLM districts respectively (U.S. Department of the Interior 1978, 1979b, 1979c).

12. East Socorro (U.S. Department of the Interior 1979c:i); East Roswell (U.S. Department of the Interior 1979c:i); Rio Puerco (U.S. Department of the Interior 1978:111-157).

13. Fifty-eight percent is the increase from the current licensed use of 58,284 animal unit months (AUMs) to the estimated grazing capacity of 91,149 AUMs by the year 2000 (U.S. Department of the Interior 1978:111-157). Fifty-seven percent is the increase from the current licensed use of 233,885 AUMs to the bureau's estimate of 367,389 AUMs available by the year 2000 (U.S. Department of the Interior 1979b:1-5).

14. The uncertainty of the estimates is reflected in the bureau's predictions and proposed actions (see U.S. Department of the Interior 1979b:1-5–1-10).

15. Allotment files in the Albuquerque District BLM office reveal coordination problems. Of the thirteen community files examined (out of thirty-four), six contained reports of disputes among permittees on maintenance, and eleven contained reports of trespass violations due to poor fencing.

16. Ranch sales data, Federal Land Bank and Western Farm Management Corporation, Albuquerque, New Mexico. Ranches with state and Forest Service permits were far less common and not included in the statistical data.

17. If the test is shifted forward to 1971 or back to 1973, the results are similar, indicating that a major change in the relationship between the BLM budget and the federal budget occurred in the early 1970s.

18. Correspondence of the author with Mr. Keith Miller, Rangelands Management Division, BLM, Washington, D.C., October 1979.

19. Correspondence of the author with Mr. David Little, Rangelands Management Division, BLM, Washington, D.C., October 1979.

BIBLIOGRAPHY

Barnett, Harold J., and Chandler Morse. 1963. *Scarcity and Growth, The Economies of Natural Resource Availability*. Baltimore: Johns Hopkins University Press.

Box, Thadis W. 1978. "The Arid Lands Revisited—One Hundred Years Since John Wesley Powell." Fifty-Seventh Annual Honor Lecture, Utah State University, Logan, Utah.

Calef, Wesley. 1960. *Private Grazing and Public Lands: Local Management of the Taylor Grazing Act*. Chicago: University of Chicago Press.

Chow, G.C. 1960. "Tests of Equality Between Subsets of Coefficients in Two Linear Regressions." *Econometrica*, pp. 591–605.

Clawson, Marion. 1971. *The Bureau of Land Management*. New York: Praeger Publications.

Cook, C.W., and P.L. Sims. 1975. "Drought and Its Relationship to Dynamics of Primary Productivity and Production of Grazing Animals." Addis Adaba: International Livestock Center for Africa.

Foss, Phillip O. 1960. *Politics and Grass*. Seattle: University of Washington Press.

Fowler, John M., and James R. Gray. 1980. *Market Values of Federal Grazing Permits in New Mexico*. Report 2, Cooperative Extension Service, Range Improvement Task Force, New Mexico State University, Los Cruces.

Gardner, B. Delworth. 1962. "Transfer Restrictions and Misallocation in Grazing Public Range." *American Journal of Agricultural Economics* 44, no. 1 (February):50–63.

Godfrey, E. Bruce. 1972. "Rangeland Improvement Practices in Idaho." Forest, Wildlife, and Range Experiment Station Information Series No. 1. Moscow: University of Idaho.

Laitala, Lee M. 1975. *BLM Advisory Boards Past, Present, and Future*. Division of Cooperative Relations, Bureau of Land Management.

Le Houerou, H.N., and C.H. Hoste. 1977. "Rangeland Production and Annual Rainfall Relations in the Mediterranean Basin and in the African Sohelo-Sudanian Zone." *Journal of Range Management* 30, no. 3 (May):181–189.

Lindsay, Cotton M. 1975. "A Theory of Government Enterprise." *Journal of Political Economy* 84, no. 5:1061–1077.

Niskanen, William A. 1971. *Bureaucracy and Representative Government*. Chicago: Aldine.

Peltzman, Sam. 1976. "Toward a More General Theory of Regulation." *Journal of Law and Economics* 19:211–240.

Pinchot, Gifford. 1947. *Breaking New Ground.* New York: Harcourt, Brace and Jovanovich.

Quirk, James P. 1976. *Intermediate Microeconomics.* Palo Alto, Ca.: Science Research Associates.

Stevens, Joe B., and E. Bruce Godfrey. 1972. "Use Rates, Resource Flows, and Efficiency of Public Investment in Range Improvements." *American Journal of Agricultural Economics* 54, no. 4 (November).

Tullock, George. 1965. *The Politics of Bureaucracy.* Washington, D.C.: Public Affairs Press.

U.S. Department of Agriculture and U.S. Department of the Interior. 1977. *Study of Fees for Grazing Livestock on Federal Lands.*

U.S. Department of Commerce. 1930-1979. *U.S. Census.*

U.S. Department of the Interior. 1950-1965. *Annual Reports* of the Secretary of the Interior.

U.S. Department of the Interior. 1950-1965. *Annual Reports* of the Director of the Bureau of Land Management.

U.S. Department of the Interior, Bureau of Land Management. 1962-1976. *Public Land Statistics.*

————. 1975. *Effects of Livestock Grazing on Wildlife, Watershed, Recreation, and Other Resource Values in Nevada.*

————. 1978. *The Proposed Rio Puerco Livestock Grazing Management Program.*

————. 1979a. *Managing the Public Rangelands.*

————. 1979b. *East Roswell Draft Grazing Environmental Statement.*

————. 1979c. *East Socorro Grazing Environmental Statement.*

U.S. General Accounting Office, Comptroller General. 1977. *Public Rangelands Continue to Deteriorate.*

U.S. House of Representatives. 1969. Committee on Interior and Insular Affairs, Subcommittee on Public Lands. *Review of Grazing Fees.* 91st Cong., 1st sess.

————. 1974. Committee on Interior and Insular Affairs. *Report on HR 5441 to Provide for the Management, Protection, Development, and Sale of the National Resource Lands.* 93rd Cong., 2d sess.

————. 1975. Committee on Interior and Insular Affairs, Subcommittee on Public Lands. *Report on the Public Land Policy and Management Act.* 94th Cong., 1st sess.

————. 1976. Committee on Interior and Insular Affairs. *Report on the Federal Land Policy and Management Act of 1976, HR 13777.* 94th Cong., 2d sess.

U.S. Senate. 1964a. Committee on Interior and Insular Affairs, Subcommittee on Public Lands. *Hearings on HR 5159 Classification and Multiple Use Act.* 88th Cong., 2d sess.

_____. 1964b. Committee on Interior and Insular Affairs. *Report on the Public Land Law Review Commission Act HR 8070.* 88th Cong., 2d sess.

_____. 1969. Committee on Interior and Insular Affairs. *Hearings on the National Environmental Policy Act S 1075.* 91st Cong., 1st sess.

_____. 1971. Environmental Policy Division, Congressional Research Service, Library of Congress, Committee on Interior and Insular Affairs. *Congress and the Nation's Environment.* 92nd Cong., 1st sess.

_____. 1975. Committee on Interior and Insular Affairs, Subcommittee on Environment and Land Resources. *Management of Natural Resource Lands.* 94th Cong., 1st sess.

Vale, Thomas R. 1975. "Presettlement Vegetation in the Sagebrush-Grass Area of the Intermountain West." *Journal of Range Management* 28, no. 1 (January):32–36.

Voigt, William, Jr. 1976. *Public Grazing Lands.* New Brunswick, N.J.: Rutgers University Press.

Youngblood, B., and A.B. Cox. 1922. "An Economic Study of a Typical Ranching Area on the Edwards Plateau of Texas." Texas Agricultural Experiment Station *Bulletin 297.*

7 A CALL FOR PRIVATE PROPERTY RIGHTS TO THE RANGE

Two highly conflicting priorities clash: keeping a maximum amount of the wilderness pure; and using America's resources for continued growth and prosperity. Weighing the relative merits is a task to daunt the most visionary planner. But it is clear that a lot of land is being "withdrawn" or closed to development, with little or no consideration being given to what resource riches it may contain.

Wall Street Journal (1979)

Efforts to assign private property rights to federal land in the 1980s reflect both a continuation of conditions which began in the 1880s and conflict between market and bureaucratic allocation of resources. This study has shown that tenure to millions of acres of rangeland has been generally insecure. That insecurity has been due to federal policies, importantly molded by the self-interest needs of the Interior Department and its agencies, the General Land Office and the Bureau of Land Management. In the nineteenth century, congressional programs to allot federal land in 160-acre parcels and the desire of the General Land Office to safeguard its role and budget effectively blocked the assignment of title to arid land. Stock owners who first settled the high plains and intermountain basins of the West commonly needed in excess of a thousand acres for viable ranches, but they could not formalize their claims. Their informal holdings were vulnerable to both new settlers in search of land and the Interior Department in administering land laws. The department opposed liberalizing the statutes and removed fences which defined claims and controlled entry and land use. Common property conditions inevitably emerged and predictable overgrazing followed.

In the twentieth century, Interior efforts to expand bureaucratic regulation, enhancing budget and staffing prospects for the BLM, have attenuated the grazing privileges of ranchers on federal land. Grazing permits, granted under the Taylor Grazing Act of 1934, initially recognized existing land use practices and provided ranchers with the first formal definition of their land claims. Relatively broad and secure at first, the privileges conveyed by the permits have been eroded by the Bureau of Land Management following controversial agency allegations of land misuse by ranchers. Charges of range deterioration from overgrazing have provided the justification for bureaucratic land use controls and sharp increases in congressional funding for scientific range management and rehabilitation. While range deterioration statistics have been incorporated in recent legislation, there is little evidence that permittees have exacerbated conditions. BLM lands have been historically among the poorest in the continental U.S., continually subject to wind and water erosion. Recent research by Vale (1975) points out that the land has never been characterized by thick grass stands. Hence, existing conditions likely reflect long-standing trends. Available research indicates that efforts by the BLM to alter those trends through investments in brush removal, plowing, and reseeding have had low returns relative to the opportunity costs of the funds involved (Stevens and Godfrey 1972). There is no reason to expect that the much larger rehabilitation programs embodied in the allotment management plans will have more favorable rates of return. Accordingly, actions to restore the range to hypothetical past conditions, which perhaps never existed, may advance the welfare of BLM personnel, but reduce social production and wealth.

That conclusion underscores the fundamental flaws of the current institutional arrangement for managing federal rangelands. That arrangement relies on bureaucratically assigned use rights which encourage inefficient land use for a number of reasons: First, since bureaucrats do not hold property rights to the range resource, they do not bear the costs nor receive the benefits of their actions and, hence, can ignore market signals and engage in socially wasteful land management policies. Second, the rights assigned are inherently tenuous since bureaucrats reallocate rangeland and readjust use privileges to meet changing political conditions. The impact of bureaucratic controls is shown in the relative decline, since the 1970s, of ranch sales prices which include BLM land and appraisal values of BLM grazing permits. Bureau regulations and uncertainty regarding future conditions have led prospective buyers to heavily discount BLM lands. Finally, conflict between ranchers and BLM officials appears to have led to reduced investment in land improvements.

These disturbing conditions point to the need for secure private property rights to the western range. Private property rights are essential for long-term decision making regarding investment in improvements, stocking practices, and land allocation. Those profit maximizing decisions of ranchers also maximize the net social value of rangeland and its contribution to production. There appear to be no significant external effects from private range use and, hence, ranchers (unlike bureaucrats) incur the full social costs and benefits from their efforts. Moreover, transaction costs in transferring land to others are likely low, encouraging transfer to those who anticipate higher returns from ownership. Active markets exist with institutional arrangements for advertising sales and purchase offers, for appraising land values, and for securing capital. These conclusions regarding the importance of secure tenure for optimal use of rangeland and other resources are supported by related research. For example, Bottomly (1963) finds more investment in irrigation and crops and less overgrazing on private than on public land in Libya. Libecap and Johnson (1980) conclude that the confused nature of grazing rights on the Navajo Reservation is a major cause of low per capita livestock-based income. Johnson and Libecap (1980) also find that the extent of overgrazing across nineteen southwestern Indian reservations varies directly with grazing rights arrangements. Where formal permits exist, the range is less intensively grazed; but where they are missing, overstocking is common. Both studies of Indian reservations point out the importance of recognizing existing users in assigning formal rights. Throughout southwestern reservations the Bureau of Indian Affairs (BIA) has attempted to redistribute rangeland when issuing permits without compensating those holding prior appropriation claims. The predictable reaction and resistance to the scheme has halted the BIA's efforts to formally control land use.

These lessons can be applied to BLM lands. Assigning title to existing permittees is the least costly way of granting private property rights. Title can be subsequently traded at low cost to others (including conservation and wildlife groups). Limited areas of great amenity value, where exclusion is for some reason difficult, can be retained under state or federal control. However, most of the 174 million acres administered by the Bureau of Land Management are not affected by those strict conditions and are amenable to private ownership. Recognizing existing uses of the range in assigning title is consistent with U.S. and state policies which have historically recognized prior appropriation claims for water, farmland, and hard-rock minerals.

Well-defined private rights capture individual incentive and initiative for using rangeland efficiently. Further, they insure response by profit-maximizing land owners to changing market demands for range use. Finally, they allow the U.S. to avoid socially costly scientific management programs advocated by the BLM. Private property rights are the necessary conditions for restoring and maintaining the productive value of a land area larger than New England and the Mid-Atlantic states combined which has been much maligned and fought over for one hundred years.

BIBLIOGRAPHY

Bottomly, Anthony. 1963. "The Effect of Common Ownership of Land upon Resource Allocation in Tripolitonia." *Land Economics* 39:91–95.

Johnson, Ronald N., and Gary D. Libecap. 1980. "Agency Costs and the Assignment of Property Rights: The Case of Southwestern Indian Reservations." *Southern Economic Journal* 47, no. 2 (October):332–347.

Libecap, Gary D., and Ronald N. Johnson. 1980. "Legislating Commons: The Navajo Tribal Council and the Navajo Range." *Economic Inquiry* 18, no. 1 (January):69–86.

Stevens, Joe B., and E. Bruce Godfrey. 1972. "Use Rates, Resource Flows, and Efficiency of Public Investment in Range Improvements." *American Journal of Agricultural Economics* 54, no. 4 (November):611–621.

Vale, Thomas R. 1975. "Presettlement Vegetation in the Sagebrush-Grass Area of the Intermountain West." *Journal of Range Management* 28, no. 1 (January):32–36.

Wall Street Journal, 18 June 1979.

INDEX

ABOUT THE AUTHOR

Gary D. Libecap received his B.A. from the University of Montana and his M.A. and Ph.D. from the University of Pennsylvania. He is currently associate professor of economics at Texas A & M University. His general interests are in the development and role of property rights institutions in natural resource management and use.

Dr. Libecap has taught economics at Midwestern University (1971-72) and Drexel University (1975-76); and been an associate for Seminars in Economic History and Legal and Economic Change, Columbia University; assistant professor of economics, Rutgers University (1976-77), and the University of New Mexico (1977-79); and visiting staff member at Los Alamos Scientific Laboratory (1979).

He is the author of *The Evolution of Private Mineral Rights*, plus articles and reviews in such scholarly journals as *Business History Review*, *Economic Inquiry*, *Explorations in Economic History*, *Journal of Economic History*, and the *Southern Economic Journal*.